PALISADES PARK PUBLIC LIBRARY
257 SECOND STREET
PALISADES PARK NJ 07650
201-585-4150

BIOG POWELL
Colin Powell : a man of war and peace
Senna, Carl, 1944- 39153050187477
Palisades Park Public Library ug 23 2019

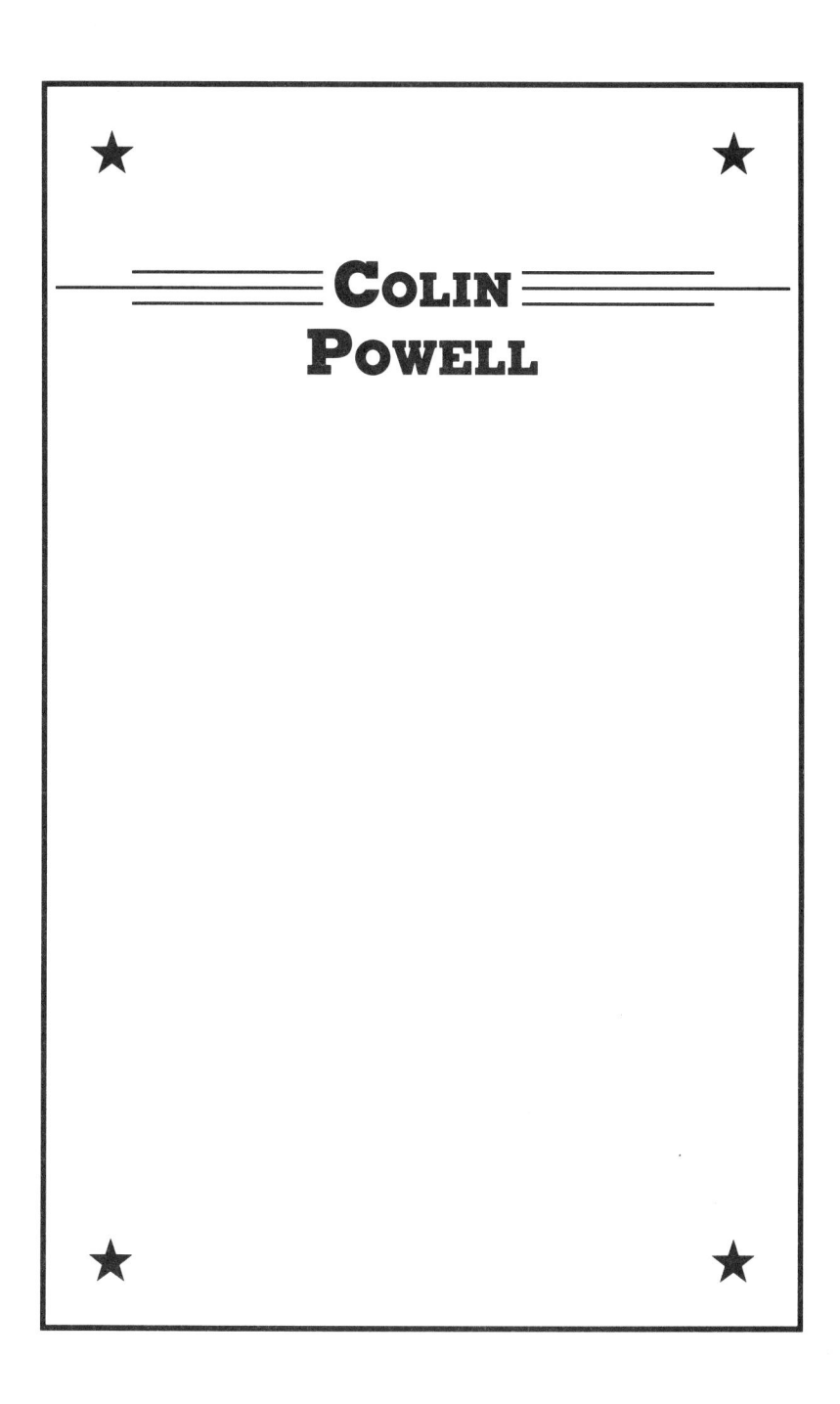

Colin Powell

COLIN POWELL

A Man of War and Peace

Carl Senna

WALKER AND COMPANY   **NEW YORK**

Copyright © 1992 by Carl Senna

All rights reserved. No part of this book may be reproduced or transmitted in any form or by any means, electronic or mechanical, including photocopying, recording, or by any information storage and retrieval system, without permission in writing from the Publisher.

First published in the United States of America in 1992 by Walker Publishing Company, Inc.

Published simultaneously in Canada by Thomas Allen & Son Canada, Limited, Markham, Ontario

Library of Congress Cataloging-in-Publication Data
Senna, Carl, 1944–
Colin Powell : a man of war and peace / Carl Senna.
   p. cm.
Summary: Examines the life and career of the Army general who became the first black chairman of the Joint Chiefs of Staff.
ISBN 0-8027-8180-2 —ISBN 0-8027-8181-0 (R)
1. Powell, Colin L.—Juvenile literature. 2. Generals—United States—Biography—Juvenile literature.
3. Afro-American generals—
Biography—Juvenile literature. 4. United States. Army—Biography—Juvenile literature. [1. Powell, Colin L. 2. Generals. 3. Afro-Americans—Biography.] I. Title.
E840.5.P68S46 1992
355'.0092—dc20
[B]   92-16099
    CIP
    AC

Book Design by Georg Brewer

Printed in the United States of America

2 4 6 8 10 9 7 5 3 1

*For Ann Lucien,
Danzy Maria, Maceo Carl,
and two soldiers with heart,
Tommy and Amos*

Contents

ACKNOWLEDGMENTS .... ★ ix
1. GROWING UP IN NEW YORK CITY .... ★ 1
2. FROM COLLEGE STUDENT TO MILITARY MAN ... ★ 12
3. THE TWO-FRONTED WAR .... ★ 21
4. MILITARY LIFE AND WORK .... ★ 29
5. BACK IN WASHINGTON .... ★ 41
6. NATIONAL SECURITY ADVISER .... ★ 53
7. NEXT STOP: THE PENTAGON .... ★ 64
8. JUST CAUSE IN PANAMA .... ★ 74
9. OPERATION DESERT SHIELD .... ★ 86
10. THE PATH TO WAR AND PEACE .... ★ 100
11. A MAN FOR ALL SEASONS .... ★ 112
   CHRONOLOGICAL SUMMARY .... ★ 121
   SOURCE NOTES .... ★ 125
   SELECTED BIBLIOGRAPHY .... ★ 137
   INDEX .... ★ 145

★ Acknowledgments ★

For supplying documents, biographical material, and photographs about himself and his family, I wish to thank General Colin Powell. I am grateful to Marilyn Berns, General Powell's sister, for sharing anecdotes and personal information about the general and about family life in the Bronx in the 1940s. Also of tremendous help were members of General Powell's staff: Caroline Pfeiffer, Colonel William Smullen III, and Captain Robin Crum. Thanks are also due the Right Reverend Stanford Chambers of St. Margaret's Church in the Bronx, Rick Hampson and Paula Vogel of Associated Press in New York, and Bernie Sullivan, editor of the *Fall River Herald*. Mrs. Barbara Farrell of the Providence College Library and the staff at the University of Connecticut at Storrs Library, the West Hartford Public Library, and the Library of Southeastern Massachusetts provided invaluable assistance.

I also would like to thank my editor, Henry Rasof, for his patience and encouragement and, last but not least, Pam Lewis for her moral support.

1

★

Growing Up in New York City

★

LUTHER THEOPHILUS POWELL, A BROWN-SKINNED man with a serious face, arrived in New York City on a passenger ship from St. Elizabeth's parish, Jamaica, in the fall of 1925. Jamaica, like other islands under British control, offered limited employment and poor living conditions for blacks, and many Jamaican immigrants ended up in New York City searching for a better life.

In Manhattan, Luther was scarcely off the boat before he was asked by an official to state his nationality. "Jamaican," he replied. But the official wrote, "African, black," a racial classification, not a nationality.[1] Like many West Indians, Luther found the United States, with its emphasis on racial, rather than national, ancestry for all blacks, both bewildering and intimidating. Jamaicans proudly identified themselves as Jamaicans, but on the island of Manhattan, Jamaicans were no longer a majority. For many though, to be a black minority in the United States was still better than life on a poor island under colonial rule.

The next year, another Jamaican, Maud Ariel

McKoy of Westmoreland township, sailed into New York City. Maud's mother had written from Cuba earlier in the year, asking Maud to join her there. Many Jamaicans worked in Cuba's capital, Havana, a city bustling with cigar and clothing factories. But Maud had heard of the perils and hardships in Havana. Not only were the wages low and the work hours long but she would also have to learn to speak Spanish. Havana, in her opinion, had none of New York's exciting opportunities. Maud dug in her heels and refused to join her mother in Cuba, telling her, "I'll only join you if you move to New York City."[2]

A heated exchange of letters passed between Maud and her mother. In the end, her mother relented and shortly after Maud arrived in Havana, they sailed from Cuba to New York City. Like Luther Powell, Maud had left Jamaica in search of a better life.

By 1927, Luther was working at various factory jobs in Connecticut. Most of the work he found was temporary or seasonal, and he was seldom away from New York for more than a month or so. Maud and her mother worked as seamstresses in Harlem. On Sundays, when Luther was in New York, he regularly attended St. Phillip's Episcopal Church in Harlem. The church held picnics during the summer at Pelham Bay Park. At one of the picnics in the summer of 1927, Luther finally got up the courage to introduce himself to Maud. A year and a half later they were engaged.

Luther and Maud began working in the garment district of Manhattan while they were engaged. On December 28, 1929, two months after the stock-market crash of October 27, 1929, they got married. For two weeks, they vacationed along the Connecticut shore. When they returned to New York after the honeymoon, however, they found that the companies they worked for had gone bankrupt. Like millions of other Americans, they were out of work almost overnight.

Luther and Maud lived in Harlem at 20 Morningside Avenue, one of a modest row of apartment buildings. In the 1920s and 1930s, few people of color lived anywhere else other than Harlem. White and black New Yorkers lived in segregated neighborhoods, and a person's color defined and decided what job, what neighborhood, and what kind of life the person had. When the Powells moved to Harlem, nearly 50,000 West Indians resided there.

Not only did West Indians vary in accents, religion, and customs from island to island—a person from Barbados easily recognized someone from Jamaica—but they differed in significant ways from other blacks. Many Jamaicans had belonged to the Anglican Church—the Church of England—in Jamaica. They ate foods unfamiliar to most American blacks: mangoes, papaws, gingerroot, plantains, pepper sauce, and goat meat. They played and sang calypso music. But the most distinctive Jamaican trait was the dialect. Luther and Maud spoke English with a British accent and a lilting, rolling sound.

The Powells were living in Harlem when a

daughter, Marilyn, was born in 1931. A second child, Colin Luther (he prefers the pronunciation "Cōlŏn," as in "semicolon"), was born five and a half years later, on April 5, 1937.

The family was deeply religious, and both Marilyn and Colin were baptized at Harlem's St. Phillip's Episcopal Church. The Powells were of a proud, ambitious group of West Indians who worked hard to become financially secure and independent. In Harlem it was often said that when a Jamaican got "ten cents above a beggar" he invested it in a business, in his family, or in a profession. And in Harlem one-third of the doctors, dentists, and lawyers were of West Indian ancestry. As a group within black America, West Indians generally shunned all forms of public welfare and public housing. Some American blacks both scorned and envied West Indian blacks for their prosperity, but most black Americans welcomed the newcomers as cousins who would contribute to black progress in America.

In 1942, the Powells moved from Harlem to the South Bronx (the Bronx is another borough of New York City), first to Fox Street and within a year to Kelly Street "for the good schools," recalled Powell.[3] Education meant a great deal to the Powells. Maud, unlike Luther, had graduated from high school, and when she differed with him on some matter, she pointedly reminded him who had a diploma and who did not. The family had moved up socially, at least in terms of general New York attitudes about neighborhoods. Because of racial discrimination in housing, most black families had little alternative to living in Harlem. An integrated South Bronx neighborhood seemed more appealing to the Powells than segregated Harlem. They wanted to continue to rise toward financial security and a better life.

At 952 Kelly Street, a four-story brick building of eight apartments, the Powells occupied the third floor. At various times, grandparents, aunts, and uncles shared the four-bedroom apartment, and during World War II they shared ration coupons for food. According to Powell, the family had "so many other cousins around that it really was sort of a floating family of lots of cousins who were almost like siblings to us all, and all of the parents of this extended family were pretty much the same."[4]

The South Bronx that Colin Powell knew in the 1940s offered, for families of moderate means, thousands of comfortable brownstone apartments and neat rows of single-family houses—cozy redbrick structures with peaked roofs, garages, and lawns. It also offered fancy houses for the more well-to-do. There were none of the slum tenements of today. People of different backgrounds generally lived in social harmony. Said Marilyn, "The neighborhood was like a small town. Everybody looked out for each other. We could never get into trouble. Everywhere you went there were forty pairs of eyes watching you."[5]

For the Powells, the South Bronx was not an environment to be ashamed of, and for Colin, "growing up there proved that it is possible to rise above conditions."[6]

Powell never knew what a "majority" race or ethnic group was while growing up. In the South Bronx, he told a reporter, "you were either black, Puerto Rican, Jewish or of some strange European extraction." On Kelly Street, "everybody was a 'minority.' "[7] A small number of blacks, including the Powells, lived among mainly Jews, Irish, and Italians, the most populous and longest-established groups. At that time racial tensions sometimes flared in other parts of New York, especially in Harlem, but not in the South Bronx's Kelly Street neighborhood.

Kelly Street offered picturesque shops, such as Kaiserman's bakery, Sammy the shoemaker's place, a storefront synagogue, and a printing shop. Around the corner were J. Sickser's children's store, Prospect Hospital, the Tiffany Theater, Public School 39, the elevated train line, and the Intervale Street subway stop. The air was filled with smells of exotic foods and a babel of foreign languages. Far from viewing the hustle and bustle of New York as unsettling, the Powells and other immigrants saw the city as a promised land.

When the Powell children started grade school at P.S. 39, their mother stayed at home. But Colin and Marilyn came home each day to find their mother, a seamstress, busy sewing clothes in the kitchen for a Manhattan garment company. "Every Thursday night," recalled Powell, he watched his mother "put those little tickets together—she did piecework—so that on Friday morning she could bundle them all up and take them down to Thirty-fourth Street and get her pay."[8]

Maud did work for the garment company at home, but her husband marched off to Gaines & Co., later Ginzberg & Co., where he worked as a shipping clerk for twenty-three years. Every weekday, Colin's father rose before dawn to dress and eat breakfast before taking the subway to the garment district.

The Powells were hardworking people. Colin's father was gone all day, every day, and he never came home before seven or eight at night. The modestly educated Maud and Luther set an example for their children and for the younger members of their extended immigrant family with their selflessness. They worked hard not for themselves but for their family, and nearly every penny they earned went to support their children. They were driven by the values they had acquired in Jamaica and by the fact that they were immigrants, and, like so many other immigrants, they worked very hard to establish themselves in their new country. Two major events that influenced them and millions of other Americans were the Depression and, of course, World War II, whose action and aftermath dominated the 1940s.

The Powells were also disciplined and religious. They strongly identified themselves with British cultural values and institutions. They were book lovers and devout members of the Episcopal, or "high," church—the American equivalent of the

Anglican church. "The higher the better," Colin once said. He found the emphasis on liturgy and ritual, with its incense and chants, its "smells and bells," very satisfying. As a boy, he served as an acolyte (altar boy) at St. Margaret's Episcopal Church on 151st Street, where his father was an official.

On Kelly Street, Colin and dozens of kids played stickball, raced bicycles and go-carts, ate hot dogs and hamburgers at a local White Castle, and paid twenty-five cents on Saturdays to watch western movies at the Tiffany Theater.

Colin was by all accounts an active child. One day when he was six years old, he saw his mother pushing his sister Marilyn on a swing in Hunt's Point Park. Colin waited for his turn. Marilyn, however, was not about to give up her seat soon enough for her younger brother. He rushed in front of the swing, striking his head against the seat and suffering a gash that required stitches. Although he never cried while being attended, the wound left a permanent scar.

Colin skipped a grade in elementary school. His command of the English language contrasted with that of many of his first-generation-immigrant classmates. Marilyn and Colin had learned to speak standard American English, only rarely exposing their roots with a lilting West Indian accent. Colin's teachers saw that he belonged with more advanced English-speaking pupils. At Intermediate School 52, Colin was considered very bright, scoring mostly eighties and nineties on tests. He was exceptionally neat and well groomed, and generally typed his reports. He also collected stamps, excelled at map drawing and French, and was elected "class captain," a rank denoting superior maturity and good behavior in his homeroom class.

Despite Colin's apparent success in elementary school, his sister Marilyn describes him as an "average or not quite average" student in school. She "was the one who was always asking" her mother to read street signs to her and spell words when they were out for a walk. Colin, according to Marilyn, "could not have cared less. . . . He was a tagalong brother" and "was a late bloomer . . . a pretty average boy." Nevertheless, she added that Colin always "had a sense of direction," and she was later surprised only by the magnitude of his achievements, not that he would succeed.[9]

Colin impressed adults as being a reflective youth who was curious and attentive to detail. The Powell family's values and Colin's own self-discipline may have played a role in helping him keep "his nose clean" of neighborhood problems. In spite of the relative stability and harmony in the South Bronx, things were beginning to change during the 1940s. The neighborhood began slowly going downhill, and more and more troubled youths could be seen idling on the streets. Colin's parents insisted on a busy and productive day as his best defense against delinquency. They also "demanded achievement" and "believed you must not waste yourself." His parents often told him,

"Strive for a good education. Make something of your life."[10]

Although Colin was uncertain what profession to choose, he was determined to accomplish something honorable that would please his parents. He knew that he did not have to become a brain surgeon or tycoon to do that. The important thing for him in school meant at least not failing his subjects. There was always an expectation that he was supposed to do better than his parents and that the key to opportunity was education. "Kids don't pick up training because parents sit around and talk to them about values," Powell once said in an interview. "Children watch their parents *live* values. Youngsters don't care what you say, but they watch what you do."[11] And the Powells had set great examples.

But even at Morris High School in the South Bronx, Colin still had no idea what he wanted to be, although he immediately joined the Morris High School track team. He worked every weekend either at J. Sickser's children's store or at odd jobs. Like many other students, Colin was eager to work to assist his family. And like many young people, Colin horsed around a lot and sometimes lagged in his studies, but he was seldom idle or engaged in mischief. Teenaged Colin overslept one morning, much to the annoyance of his mother. She had his four-year-old cousin Victor Roque awaken Colin by pouring a glass of cold water on him. Colin then chased his cousin out of the room. Said Roque in an interview, "I was either very brave for a kid or very stupid."[12]

Colin was sixteen when he graduated with average grades from Morris High in 1953. His steady progress among older, hardworking, and very intelligent schoolmates indicated precocity in terms of his mental ability. Still, if he had the means for success, he yet lacked the maturity to know what to do with his talent. His first choice for college was New York University, and his second choice was CCNY, the City College of New York.[13]

"Notwithstanding my rather mediocre high school grades," he later recalled, "I was accepted at both institutions. Making the final decision was tough, but one I was able to come to grips with readily—NYU cost $750 a year; CCNY cost $10. That was the end of that."[14]

★
From College Student to Military Man
★

TO EARN ENOUGH MONEY FOR HIS BOOKS AND clothes, Colin waited until the spring 1954 college term to enroll at CCNY, rather than in the fall of 1953. One bitterly cold morning in February 1954, he hurriedly said good-bye to his parents, not even taking time to finish his breakfast, and he climbed aboard a bus across the 155th Street bridge. As the bus approached the hill to the campus, Colin was filled with anxiety and anticipation. Suddenly he was hungry. But when he got off the bus, the first sight that greeted him was a friendly one, Raymond the Bagelman. He had discovered a campus tradition, thus beginning his career as a CCNY student.

His parents had advised him to study engineering, a popular major in the 1950s. Dutifully, he applied to the School of Engineering, passed his test, and was accepted. Colin went to college for one reason: his parents wanted him to. "I don't even remember," he once explained, "having any great urge to get a higher education. I don't even remember consciously thinking the matter through. I just recall that my parents expected it of me. And in those days when your parents expected something, it was what you had to do. In my family, especially, you did what your parents expected of you."[1]

He got through his first semester, from February to June, with a B average, but he dropped an introductory course in engineering because it seemed too advanced for him. Still hoping to become an engineer, he intended to take the course in a later term. When his second semester began in June, he took a mechanical drawing class. The weather was uncomfortably hot one afternoon, and the classroom lacked air-conditioning. As Colin began to perspire, he became distracted by the heat. Just then, his instructor asked him to describe a cone intersecting a plane in space.

Colin's mind went blank. For a few tense moments he struggled unsuccessfully to conceive of the figure. But having never drawn the cone with a plane through it, he simply was unable to represent a geometric shape without having had it first presented to him. He decided that his aptitudes lay elsewhere. His choice to drop his major in engineering made the second term "the worst summer" he had in college.[2] But his decision showed that he had a realistic assessment of his own weaknesses, though he almost always resisted quitting any task that he had set for himself. Most of all, he did not want to disappoint his parents. The idea of giving up engineering was a painful trial for someone accustomed to "winging" his studies in high school. Despite his achieving a B average the first semester, he decided in the summer term to switch to geology.

Early in his first semester he had noticed uniformed students in the Reserve Officers Training Corps (ROTC). He was attracted to the uniforms and to the sense of fraternity among the ROTC officers, especially the Pershing Rifles, a group whose members wore a little whipped cord on their shoulders. The whipped cord indicated to the freshman that members of the Pershing Rifles had status and purpose that distinguished them from the ordinary ROTC candidates.

In the fall of his first year, Colin joined ROTC and pledged Pershing Rifles. ROTC would be his main academic interest for the next four years. He hadn't planned for a military career, but now he seriously began thinking about such a career. The status of military men and women, as well as their financial security, made a career in the service very attractive to Powell. Military culture permeated American news. Positive public attitudes toward the military had been carried over from World War II to the Korean War (1950–53). And Dwight D. Eisenhower, the supreme allied commander during World War II, had been elected president of the United States in 1952.

When Colin Powell joined ROTC at CCNY, he enjoyed opportunity and freedom that blacks had recently won. Powell followed a long tradition of black Americans in the military: His entry into ROTC was forty years after Army Sgt. Benjamin O. Davis became the first black to rise from the ranks to a commissioned officer. Davis ended his career as a brigadier general. In June 1936, Davis's son, Benjamin O. Davis, Jr., became the first black cadet to graduate from West Point since 1889, and went on to become a general himself.

Although blacks had fought in every American war, beginning with the Revolutionary War in 1776, they usually found themselves excluded from the benefits of a military career, including prestige, veterans' benefits, and a good civilian job. Black troops mobilized at the start of World War II had served in segregated units. They had been permitted to fight only out of military necessity, after the Allies had been unable to win the war without them. Writing at about the time Powell entered CCNY, James Baldwin made the bitter observation on historical discrimination in the military: "That this cynical and treacherous pattern has not altered from that day to this is scarcely worth mentioning; but it is worth observing that, whereas Americans profess not to know what the [black] wants, they always know what to promise him whenever they need his body."[3]

In 1941, pressed to the wall by the threat of a march on Washington by black civil rights leaders, President Franklin D. Roosevelt signed an executive order barring segregation and discrimination in government agencies, including the military. Numerous problems continued, but by the time of the Korean War, the way had been paved for fuller participation by blacks in the military.

In 1954, the year after Powell graduated from

high school, the Supreme Court decided in *Brown v. Topeka Board of Education* to eliminate all legal support for racial segregation in public education. Thousands of blacks stood to benefit from the decision. Colin's generation, however, had suffered a severe economic recession following the Korean War. Like many young black men, Colin viewed military service as offering more advancement than civilian work could offer. Besides guaranteeing a person's paycheck, the military provided free family medical services and paid for college and professional graduate education.

While Powell was attending CCNY, the lives of blacks were at a feverish pitch. Ominous calls for black separatism echoed in the streets of many urban centers. Poet Langston Hughes's famous question—"What happens to a dream deferred? . . . Does it explode?"—reflected the anger of black radicals such as Harlem's Malcolm X of the separatist Nation of Islam. The message of that anger to Powell was that he must make America live up to America's constitutional promises. At CCNY, however, Colin experienced no significant discrimination.

Colin worked hard at being a good officer cadet. His ROTC unit had mostly Jewish cadets and few blacks. Interestingly, because so many of his South Bronx friends and employers had been Jewish, Colin spoke some Yiddish. But the fraternal aspects of ROTC and the glamour of the uniform mattered less to him than the duty attached to it. In his second year at CCNY, he also realized that ROTC was fun, and he did it well.[4] Mitchell Strear, Powell's cousin and ROTC classmate, recalled: "Even back then Colin drew attention when he entered a room. At the age of eighteen, his bearing, manner, and presence were special. You just knew he would become a leader. The infantry has a motto: 'Follow me.' Colin's manner of acceptance of responsibility and leadership all said 'Follow me.' "[5]

While in ROTC, Colin took summer training at Fort Bragg, North Carolina, which, despite various court rulings, was still very much segregated. It was his first experience with legal segregation. He saw signs requiring the races to use separate rest rooms in bus and train stations and excluding blacks from motels and restaurants. He was angered by what he saw. Despite his opposition to segregation, his Army status prevented him from actively joining the civil rights protests at the time.

Powell's attitude toward the racism he saw then was "not to worry about it." He knew he could not "change the hearts and minds of people." All he expected to do was the best he could alone to fight racism. His attitude, as he expressed it in an interview, was:

> You put me anywhere into the game with you, and if the ground is reasonably level (it doesn't have to be perfectly level; it never has been), I am going to beat you at it and I am going to beat you at it because I am going to do better than you are. . . . If you are going to beat me, you are not going to beat me because I am of the wrong color; you are going to beat me

because you are better than me, because you prepared yourself better. . . . What I can't accept are young people who when they go into that kind of competition go in saying, well, I am going to lose. I am going to lose because I am from the inner city; or I am going to lose because I once was on drugs; or I am going to lose because I came from a broken home; or I am going to lose because I am black; or I am going to lose because I am white. . . . Just don't accept that kind of attitude. Don't allow yourself to be put in that kind of a position. You go in saying, I am going to win because I prepared myself better and if you are going to beat me, you are going to beat me on performance, not anything else. But then you have to take the next critical step . . . which is to prepare yourself better and not hide behind some disadvantage you have found in your background that gives you a loser's attitude going in. If you have a loser's attitude going in, you will come out a loser.[6]

By the time Powell graduated, on June 9, 1958, with a bachelor's degree in geology, he had risen to the rank of cadet colonel and been named a "distinguished military graduate." His grades? C average in academic subjects and straight A's in ROTC. He had done ROTC proud and he enjoyed it.

After graduation, Powell decided that his best option was to join the army, even though he would have been almost immediately drafted anyway. He accepted a commission as a second lieutenant in the infantry at sixty dollars a week and went to Fort Benning, Georgia, where he continued his military education. Although Powell had not graduated from West Point—almost an informal requirement for promotion to general in the army—he had received a solid education at CCNY and could compete with the best cadets from West Point.

His parents supported and even encouraged his decision, since it was unlikely that he would escape the draft, which then required two years of service for every able-bodied man between the ages of eighteen and thirty-five. His parents believed that he would fulfill his military obligation in a couple of years, while obtaining further training and skills. They expected that after completing his tour of duty he would come home to get "a real job."[7]

His initial assignment came in October 1958, when he was sent to a troop unit in West Germany. His positions included platoon leader—leading forty men—and executive officer.

In December 1960, he was transferred to Fort Devens in Ayer, Massachusetts, where he held various positions. The proximity of Boston made it an attractive destination for weekend leave to many of the bachelors on the base, including Colin Powell, the dashing twenty-two-year-old first lieutenant. One day, he went on a date, arranged by a friend, with Alma Vivian Johnson, a beautiful student teacher from Birmingham, Alabama, who was studying audiology at Emerson College and learning to teach the hearing impaired.

Alma knew little about the military, except what she had read and heard in the media, but gentleman and officer Colin Powell swept her off her feet. He was intelligent, articulate, and gallant. She was the daughter of a high school principal and came from an old and distinguished line of educators and business professionals, part of a genteel class of southern blacks for whom a military career was less attractive than a civilian profession. Though Powell lacked her pedigree, he was attractive for his exceptional personal qualities, especially his maturity, sense of responsibility, and self-confidence. She also liked the idea of the travel that went with Army life.

Two years later, on August 24, 1962, Colin Powell and Alma Johnson were married. It seemed, at first, a quiet year, but it turned out to be a year to be remembered.

3

THE TWO-FRONTED WAR

★

SOON AFTER HIS WEDDING, POWELL RECEIVED HIS marching orders. He would be sent to a small country in Southeast Asia that had been in turmoil for years. And what was he leaving? A nation becoming increasingly embroiled in a domestic turmoil of a different kind: a struggle over civil rights.

In 1954, the Vietnamese inhabitants of what was then called French Indochina threw out their French masters and formed themselves into two countries: Communist North Vietnam and pro-Western South Vietnam. A long guerrilla war ensued, during which the Communist Viet Cong, encouraged and supported by North Vietnam, sought to overthrow the regime in the south and reunite the two halves of the country. By 1962, these forces had grown so strong that the United States began to send in troops to help prop up the corrupt and ailing South Vietnamese government.

Also in 1954, a fight to the end for black civil rights began in the United States with the *Brown* v. *Topeka Board of Education* Supreme Court decision that finally paved the way for equality for blacks.

Two years later, in Montgomery, Alabama, blacks united behind the defiance of Rosa Parks (who refused to give up her seat in a segregated section of a bus) and the oratory of Martin Luther King, Jr. Boycotting the segregated buses, blacks won a court decision ending segregation of public transportation. Four students from North Carolina's black Agricultural and Technical College at Greensboro, North Carolina, started the first protest against lunch-counter segregation with a "sit-in" in 1960. In the same year, the Congress of Racial Equality challenged "Jim Crow" laws all across the South. (In the early 1800s, "Jim Crow" was the stage name of white minstrels who mocked blacks in song and dance. After the Civil War the name was used to describe any racially discriminatory laws against blacks.) The protesters encountered white violence, bus burnings, and arrest for their actions. In 1963, the same year the United States began a major commitment of troops to Vietnam, Martin Luther King, Jr., led a massive rally in Washington, D.C., and sparked legislation—the Civil Rights Act of 1964—that ended all legal forms of racial discrimination.

When Powell received his orders, his new wife, Alma, said good-bye to him at Fort Devens, and he went to Fort Bragg, North Carolina, for two months to receive further training. When he flew to Vietnam in December as a captain, his wife returned to her parents' home in Birmingham.

For Alma, home was where her "support system was."[1] But the Birmingham that Alma returned to was in an uproar over bombings and drive-by shootings at black homes. Although her parents' home was in a pleasant middle-class neighborhood, times were changing.

Birmingham was very segregated—blacks and whites lived in different parts of the city and attended separate schools and churches. The races seldom met at any public social event. Even sporting events were segregated. Then four black girls were slain in a bombing of a black church. Whites were assaulting black homes, so blacks began arming themselves. Protest organizations led groups of integrated passengers in violation of Birmingham's segregation of restaurants and bus and train stations. Many white restaurants closed down rather than seat blacks and whites together. A black voter-registration drive in the city provoked white mobs and police to violent assaults on innocent blacks.

While Alma slept at night, protected by her father with a shotgun at the ready, Powell saw action for the first time in the jungles of Vietnam. When the couple's first child, Michael, was born in 1963, Powell was deep in the swamps of Vietnam, suffering from diarrhea, mosquitoes, and leeches, and leading a combat unit under intense enemy fire near the North Vietnamese border. He did not learn of his son's birth until several weeks later.[2]

Powell assumed a different identity when he donned a uniform in Vietnam—one that was with him twenty-four hours each day. He also began to judge people almost instinctively by a different yardstick of social division from the racial and ethnic perceptions of people whom he had known in civilian life. His only loyalty was to the color of his uniform. Not that racial distinctions or racial problems disappeared, but military rank superseded all else as the primary indicator of a person's status, privilege, and authority. Powell had to acknowledge the color of bars and stars before he was even aware of the racial identity of the soldier before him. His life in Vietnam depended on it.

During this time, many blacks, especially blacks in the military, noticed the irony of the black man's defending his country's interests and the "freedom" of nonwhite Asians in a faraway land when at home he couldn't even sit where he wanted to on a bus. Faced with legal racism off the base, black soldiers attempted, if in some cases grudgingly, to grin and bear the bitter irony.

One day, while Powell was leading a patrol deep into enemy held territory, he was wounded by the Viet Cong. As the unit was passing through a rice paddy, Powell stepped on a punji-stick, a Viet Cong booby trap, which pierced his left foot through his boot. He had to be evacuated to a base hospital in the South Vietnamese city of Hué for surgery and stitches. He received a Purple Heart for his injury. Although many wounded men saw an injury as an automatic transfer back to the States and the chance to fill out their careers in noncombat desk duty, Powell was determined to complete his yearlong tour of active combat service. His wound healed in a few weeks, and he returned to action as an adviser to a South Vietnamese infantry battalion.

After nearly a year in Vietnam, Powell returned to Fort Benning, enriched by a Purple Heart and a Bronze Star for valor, the two highest Army awards for a soldier. Although Powell had been in Vietnam during the summer of 1963, the South and Birmingham had been on his mind. "My family lived in Birmingham that terrible summer of 1963," Powell said. When he returned, he "was hit full force with what had happened in my absence. I was stunned, disheartened, and angry. While I had been fighting in Vietnam alongside brave soldiers trying to preserve their freedom, in my own land a long-simmering conflict had turned into an open fight in our streets and cities—a fight that had to be won."[3]

For a few months after Colin's return from Vietnam, Alma continued to live in Birmingham, taking care of son Michael under the care of her parents. Colin was stationed at Fort Benning, Georgia, waiting to receive his new assignment and housing suitable for his family. He commuted weekends for a few months to be with Alma and their child. Being accustomed to an integrated military life in Vietnam, where American brass stressed racial harmony, Colin was uncomfortable in Birmingham. The city was experiencing almost daily racial violence.

When the family was again reunited under the same roof, they lived in base housing, a place Alma thought "wonderful," despite its barracks-like simplicity. With a toddler, Alma was at home most of the time. Although there was little time to work on her master's degree, she found the military environment "comfortable."

The Powells were described by all who knew them as a loving team, and Alma proved to be an indispensable player. Because of Colin's career, she was often faced with having to move at a moment's notice. The disruptions were a terrible strain on the young family, without easy access to lifelong confidants and families for moral support. But the Powells soon learned that at such times they encouraged one another better than anyone else.

In 1963, Colin had some firsthand experiences of segregation, Southern style, as he explained in 1988 to a reporter for *Ebony* magazine. In Columbus, Georgia, he attempted to buy a hamburger at a restaurant. A woman asked him if he was an African student.

"No," said Colin.

"A Puerto Rican?" she asked.

"No."

"You're Negro?" she asked.

"That's right."

"Well, I can't bring out a hamburger," she said. "You'll have to go to the back door." Colin refused the offer.

"I wasn't even trying to do a sit-in," he later recalled. "All I wanted was a hamburger."[4]

When the Civil Rights Act was signed about five months later, Colin made it a point of pride to go back to the restaurant and be served a hamburger.

That same year, he was traveling in "a little German Volkswagen with New York license plates. On the back bumper was an 'All the Way with LBJ' bumper sticker on it." As he passed through Sylacauga, Alabama, he accelerated well above the speed limit. He was overdue for a meeting at Fort Benning across the Georgia-Alabama border. A white Alabama state patrol officer clocked him going at 70 miles per hour and stopped him. The policeman handed him a Goldwater for President sticker and inspected his car, its New York license plate, and the LBJ sticker. Colin waited with his heart pounding hard. The suspense was almost unbearable. His wife had warned him of the dangers facing blacks from southern white policemen. Finally the policeman said: "Boy, get out of here. You are not smart enough to hang around."[5]

After working at various assignments at Fort Benning over the next few years and being promoted to major in 1966, Powell was assigned to Fort Leavenworth, Kansas, in 1967. His time at Fort Benning had been instructive, teaching him how to manage departmental budgets as well as soldiers, and in an interview he attributed all he knows about soldiering and basic officer infantry training to that period. Fort Leavenworth, an orderly, middle-class town boasting of a frontier history, would deepen his knowledge of military leadership.[6]

Alma said she and Colin found Fort Leavenworth an "outpost of gracious living."[7] They lived in the house George Custer had occupied before he fought the Battle of Little Bighorn. At Fort Leavenworth, Powell applied to graduate school. His superior officer, who had to recommend him for that course of study, was not impressed with Colin Powell: "Your college record isn't good enough," said the officer. To a person with less self-confidence, the officer's discouraging words would have ended the application. But for Powell the officer had given him greater motivation to prove himself.[8]

Powell signed up for advanced study at the Army Command and General Staff College. When he graduated in 1968, he ranked second in a class of 1,244, a full major.

As Powell learned more about military leadership at Leavenworth, the war in Vietnam grew fierce. At home, civil rights demonstrations and anti–Vietnam War protests dominated headlines. Blacks had won major victories with the Civil Rights Act of 1964, the establishment of an Equal Opportunity Employment Commission, and the 1965 Voter Registration Act. But white attitudes and informal racist practices in employment and housing still frustrated the black search for racial equality. This frustration culminated in violent uprisings in 1967 in Newark, New Jersey, and Detroit, Michigan. National Guardsmen had to be called in to enforce peace. Detroit alone suffered forty-three deaths and millions of dollars in property damage from arson and looting.

For the Powells, the racial riots were as remote from the routine of Fort Leavenworth as was the violence in Vietnam. But that life was to be interrupted in June 1968 by another tour of duty in Vietnam for Colin Powell.

4

★
MILITARY LIFE AND WORK
★

SOON AFTER COLIN POWELL FINISHED HIS STUDIES at Fort Leavenworth in 1968, he began to receive attention from the local press. Powell's division commander saw an article in the *Army Times* newspaper featuring Powell and four other top students in the Leavenworth graduating class. The commander was astonished that he did not even know the names of his best men. "I've got the number two Leavenworth graduate in my division, and he's stuck in the boonies?" he shouted to his aides. "I want him on my staff!"[1]

In June of that year, Powell began a second tour of Vietnam. The number of American troops in Vietnam was now at the half-million mark, and Powell was again among them. He served first in the Americal Division as a battalion executive officer, where his main duties involved implementing and developing new strategies of troop training. Much like the coach of a football or basketball team, he conducted mock battle rehearsals, or war games, pitting groups of soldiers against one another in order to prepare them for real combat. Next he became the division's assistant chief of staff, responsible for combat operations of that entire unit, as well as replacing incompetent commanders who suffered too many casualties or had discipline problems among their men.[2]

No sooner had Powell landed in Vietnam than he and the rest of the nation learned of President Johnson's decision not to seek reelection. The antiwar movement had scored a major political coup. For Powell and other troops in Vietnam the angry protests and Johnson's resignation were disheartening. The American troops were fighting in a strange land for a cause they did not understand. Without the support of the American people, the troops in Vietnam found less motivation to fight. Most of the draftees simply wanted to stay alive until their one-year tour of duty was over and they could return home. Johnson's decision not to run again meant the war was going to be a stalemate; it could not be won. Powell learned the lessons of this period well—especially that a war, to be successfully prosecuted, needs the political support of the public and the Congress.

In Vietnam this time around, Powell quickly made his mark. On one helicopter mission, the pilot tried to land in a small jungle clearing. Suddenly the rotor blade hit a tree, and the chopper crashed. Powell leaped out of the smoking wreckage, only to realize that the other men were still trapped inside. Although he was nearly blinded by the smoke, he groped his way back into the tangle of steel, broken glass, and wires. The craft's fuselage was rapidly filling with combustible fumes. Powell found it increasingly hard to breathe the toxic air. At any moment he feared that the chopper could explode. The first man he found was near death—the man had been impaled through the helmet by the chopper's controls. Immediately Powell began carrying and dragging the others to a clearing safely away from the wreck. As he was carrying the last man to the clearing, the chopper exploded in a spectacular fireball. For saving the lives of the men and risking his own safety, Powell received the Soldier's Medal.

The crash was a terrible disaster, but it showed that he had healthy reflexes to danger and yet could quickly regain his self-control—the kind of soldier who, while he might be scared, would not permit himself to be paralyzed by his fear. As he put it, "There are all kinds of fears from day to day . . . anxiety in every situation . . . Yet fear is just something else that has to be dealt with and modulated. You know, the old television ad, 'Never let them see you fall.' But . . . everybody is afraid of something or other and it [fear] is an emotion you can never totally get rid of."[3]

Powell's second tour of Vietnam came as the United States was undergoing massive social change, with dramatic breakthroughs for blacks and women. But despite black progress in domestic affairs, they were carrying a disproportionate burden of the Vietnam War casualties. Although black troops made up only 11 percent of the total American fighting force, they suffered nearly 25 percent of the killed in action from 1966 to 1971. One *Time* magazine correspondent wrote in May 1967, "The [black] American is winning—indeed has won—a black badge of courage that his nation must forever honor." Nevertheless, the Army reenlistment rate in 1968 and in the early 1970s for blacks was three times that of whites.[4]

Nineteen sixty-eight had the highest number of American casualties to date. It was the year of a sensational thrust by the Viet Cong, known as the Tet Offensive. The offensive failed militarily, despite many American deaths, but it weakened American political support for the war. It made optimistic military predictions of a Viet Cong defeat—the so-called light at the end of the tunnel—seem false.

When he left Vietnam in July 1969, Colin Powell was a highly rated leader and a battle-tested officer. He also was the father of a daughter, Linda, born in 1969, not long after his return.

For Powell the worst thing about that period was not so much the protests as the absence of political commitment to win the war by military means. When the public was asked to rank professions by status, a military career fell far below the appeal of other professions. Yet the idea of sending soldiers to defend South Vietnam without providing them with the capability to defeat North Vietnam made little sense to any soldier. The result would only be more casualties and a stalemate, if not an outright loss of South Vietnam.

Powell had no doubt about the justice of America's defense of South Vietnam. Otherwise he would not have voluntarily served a second tour of hazardous duty—something rare then for a soldier with family obligations. As Powell saw the depth and extent of public division on the war, he had misgivings about leaving his family for a third tour of combat duty. He decided to remain in the states. He had always wanted to attend graduate school, so he applied to and was accepted by George Washington University in Washington, D.C. From 1970 to 1971 he divided his time between a desk job at the Pentagon and classes at George Washington University. In July 1970, he was promoted to lieutenant colonel, a position he had long aspired to.

At CCNY, he had been told, " 'If you do everything well and keep your nose clean for twenty years, we'll make you a lieutenant colonel.' That was my goal. And after twenty years, you could get a pension. In an immigrant family, that was very important."[5]

In 1971, after he earned a master's degree in business administration, he was immediately appointed operations research analyst in the Army's Office of the Assistant Vice Chief of Staff. In his new job, he helped to manage the country's defense budget and to ensure that the cost and quality of soldiers and weapons matched the needs of the president's defense strategy.

For a young military officer with fifteen years in the service and an M.B.A., Powell could have chosen a lucrative career in the Washington bureaucracy or the world of high finance. But in 1972, Powell received a telephone call from a top Army personnel officer. "Colin," the officer said, "the Infantry Branch wants one of its people to become a White House Fellow. We want you to apply."[6]

At age thirty-five, Powell applied to be a White House Fellow, one of an elite group of special assistants in a highly important government office—what Powell described as a "dream job" in the Nixon administration.[7] He was one of only seventeen people picked from 1,500 applicants. As a White House Fellow, Powell was on the other side of the executive branch, making policy and setting goals for the military defense establishment. He now would see firsthand the interrelationship between the civilian and military worlds—how, for example, foreign policy and congressional legislation affected the military budget. In the White House, Powell worked with National Security Council staff to prepare analyses showing how a tax cut could influence troop levels and military technology development.

In September 1972, Powell was assigned to the Office of Management and Budget, working under Caspar Weinberger, the director of the office, and Weinberger's Deputy, Frank C. Carlucci. Early on, Powell's superiors spotted him as a bright young comer. The three men became close friends, and the job became a turning point in Powell's life. From then on he worked in close proximity to political and civilian leadership on Capitol Hill.

The fellowship and Powell's dream job ended in August 1973. His next assignment returned him to barracks life, in September 1973, as a battalion commander in Seoul, Korea, where the United

States maintained a strong military presence to counteract any threat from North Korea or Communist China. He was directly responsible for the lives of nearly 5,000 men and women. He set policy for all work details, training exercises, promotions, salaries, equipment purchases, arbitration of disputes, and courts-martial. Though the post was hardly a dream job, it placed him where both the career pitfalls and the opportunities for advancement were greater than if he were sitting at a desk at the Pentagon, where he might have developed into a career bureaucrat. The immediate reason for his transfer had as much to do with his experience in personnel psychology and race relations as with his military training.

Under President Nixon, blacks had become increasingly strident about the end of government support for Johnson's War on Poverty and about their civil rights. Nixon and Republican party strategists devised a "southern strategy" so as to increase white southern support of the Republicans. Part of that strategy was to appear at least to be unsympathetic to black demands. The short-term effect in the black community was increased anger and despair, attitudes that found their way onto military bases.

By then, many American soldiers from Vietnam were thoroughly demoralized, and racial conflict and drug abuse were rampant. A few weeks after arriving in Korea, Powell was assigned to straighten out the 1st Battalion, a unit plagued by drugs and racial riots. Greater freedom and equality in the military had lowered the tolerance of black soldiers for racist remarks from whites. Although white racism was less oppressive in the military than in civilian life, there was enough racism—expressed in racial slurs and verbal abuse—to fuel increasing racial animosity among black troops. But for some black troops, racial confrontations became an excuse for conduct unbecoming a soldier, a reason to drink and brawl rather than expose the abuse.

To clean up the Korean battalion, Powell had to act decisively. And he was universally praised by blacks and whites for his fairness.

"I threw the bums out of the Army and put the drug users in jail," he said. "The rest, we ran four miles every morning, and by night they were too tired to get into any trouble."[8] Months later the problems in his battalion had been eliminated. Black and white troops worked comfortably together and even socialized during their free time.

Powell demonstrated that he was a problem solver in his Korean command. He learned to focus on the important issue of restoring military morale, authority, and discipline. He served in Korea for twelve months before returning to Washington. His success in Korea won him another appointment to the Pentagon in 1974. As an analyst of the Army's manpower requirements in the Office of the Assistant Secretary of Defense, his new job was to determine the training skills needed by the Army for the next decade. And for the next year Powell researched and wrote reports analyzing what educational level the next generation of missile, tank, and infantry units would need in a future defense mission.

Meanwhile Richard Nixon, under threat of impeachment, resigned in disgrace from the presidency. Nixon's vice-president, Gerald R. Ford, was sworn in as president on August 9, 1974. The abrupt change in government, with its resulting military vacancies, impressed on Powell the need for further training, so that when opportunities for advancement came along, he would be prepared to take advantage of them.

Powell began studies in advanced military schooling at Fort McNair, the National War College, in 1976, and was promoted to full colonel.

Powell's return to school and his wide readings in history and current affairs indicated the rigorous intellectual standards of leadership that he set for himself and others. In a rapidly changing world, Powell insisted on retooling his skills and keeping up with new developments in his field. As things turned out, his dedication to self-improvement and his high marks at the National War College won him a new post. For a year Powell commanded a brigade at Fort Campbell, Kentucky.

Returning again to Washington in 1977, he worked for John Kester, an assistant to the secretary of defense—the cabinet officer responsible for managing the military according to the president's and Congress's will. At their first meeting, Kester told him, "I've checked you out and what I've heard is good." Powell replied, with a wry bit of humor,

"I've checked you out and I have to tell you, it's not all good."[9]

According to Kester, Powell "did not spend time flattering people. He was just a very, very strong and wise person who understood the complexities of government. He understood people and liked them in spite of that. He was equally comfortable in the military or civilian side or when he was talking with a private, a general or a president."[10]

Because of his efficiency and genius for organization, Powell was in great demand around Washington. He was noted for rare poise and for shattering many myths about blacks "with class and elegance,"[11] wrote a reporter for *Jet* magazine in 1989. In 1979 he became a brigadier (one-star) general. In nine years he had gone beyond his earlier dream rank of lieutenant colonel.

In 1981, Powell again returned to the field, this time becoming assistant division commander of the 4th Infantry Division at Fort Carson, Colorado, a major command post of the United States Army. He was responsible for the full range of operations, for teaching approximately 18,000 soldiers how to use the tanks, artillery, and armored troop carriers of the mechanized (soldiers in driven vehicles) 4th Infantry Division.

In 1982 he became the deputy commanding general, United States Army Combined Arms Combat Development Activity, Fort Leavenworth, Kansas. At that post, he was responsible for the routine activities of the base, ordering supplies, recommending promotions and demotions, and punishing malefactors. Besides developing budgets for equipment, salaries, and benefits, he wrote a manual for teachers of air and land assault units, and operations requiring coordination of Army land troops and Air Force planes. Finally, he was acting post commander in the absence of the commander.

While jogging around the base one morning, Powell noticed Buffalo Soldier Alley. He recognized that the alley commemorated the 10th Cavalry, one of several units of black troopers who fought in the Great Plains and Indian wars to help settle the West. He knew the history well, how Native American foes had respected the tenacity and courage of the black troops so much the Indians named them Buffalo Soldiers. Powell, too, felt respect for the Buffalo Soldiers and said they deserved a more fitting monument than an alley.[12]

Powell suggested the idea of a monument to the Buffalo Soldiers. Ten years later, a committee that he helped form would raise over a half-million dollars to have a larger-than-life equestrian statue, based on a painting by Lee Brubaker, *Scout's Out*, surrounded by pools and waterfalls at Fort Leavenworth. The Brubaker painting shows a squad of black calvary officers, dressed in blue Union uniforms and accompanied by an Indian scout, patrolling a western mountain range.[13]

In 1983, while recruiting for a new military assistant, Defense Secretary Caspar Weinberger asked that Powell's name be placed on a list of people to be interviewed. After two years' absence, the bright experienced officer was sorely missed in

Washington's defense establishment. Fate seemed determined to deny him obscurity.

Because of his courage and heroism in Vietnam, he had emerged in the defense establishment with a solid reputation as a natural leader. And his personal background, sense of heritage, and ability to deal with all kinds of people made him an ideal candidate for more public policy positions. Along the way, Powell moved from one assignment to another, returning to school for additional training and education and being promoted from jobs in the field to jobs in Washington. His fast career track not only enabled him to learn the military from all angles of service and command but also nurtured a flexibility and quickness in mastering new administrative responsibilities. His "quick study" skills would come in handy in increasingly challenging positions.

5

★
BACK IN WASHINGTON
★

WEINBERGER'S INTEREST IN POWELL FOR A NEW position did not excite Powell, who was reluctant to leave the military once again to work for the Defense Department. He would have less authority and responsibility there than in a purely military position. In addition, he believed that by temperament and training his strength lay in the military rather than in the bureaucracy of Washington. Furthermore, he knew his weaknesses, one of which was his awkwardness in facing the press. Although he was capable of eloquence when the situation required it, he had never been accustomed to circumlocution.[1] And in Washington politics, being quick on one's feet with an entertaining, often meaningless pun or quote was a prerequisite, as President Reagan aptly demonstrated.

So hesitant was Powell to take the position that he almost eliminated himself from serious consideration for the post. Asked by Weinberger whether he wished to remain in the military or to work in Washington, Powell answered in favor of the former. He liked being close to his troops and felt comfortable among them.

Weinberger eventually convinced him that a strong and wise military adviser was needed by the president. Weinberger firmly believed that only Powell would fit the bill. After many meetings and discussions, Powell was persuaded that he could best serve the country by returning to Washington.

In July 1983, Powell became military adviser to Frank Carlucci, the deputy defense secretary. In August, he was promoted to major general and awarded a second star. He then went on to be the military assistant to Secretary of Defense Weinberger himself. In this position, Powell took command of the liaison office, which responds to military requests from the White House to meet crises. Being a liaison meant that Powell was the link between the national security adviser to the president and the Defense Department. At last he was in a position where he could shape the language of a presidential request and influence a military order from the White House. Likewise, he could shape a request from the Defense Department to the president. Although he was a messenger between the White House and the Defense Department, he was a very important one, for his ability to translate civilian goals into military capabilities could speed up a White House military request to meet a crisis.

In his position as Weinberger's military assistant, Powell had the duty of reporting to Weinberger the failure of administration policy in Lebanon after a terrorist attack there killed 237 U.S. Marines. Among other things, he oversaw the United States' invasion of Grenada in October 1983, was instrumental in the freeing of a Navy officer shot down over Syria, and had a key role in arms control negotiations with the former Soviets. Within the military establishment around Washington, he served as Weinberger's eyes and ears. He "gofered" the Pentagon halls, talking on the telephone, picking up any tidbits of information that he thought his boss had to have for protection from bureaucratic backstabbing.

Powell's attitude toward Weinberger and the staff was one of unflinching loyalty and fairness. But he had no illusions about human frailty. The Defense Department imposed a discipline on individuals working for it; sometimes the discipline broke down. Powell understood that people could not be expected to offer the consistent performance of machines. His staff, he knew, would be loyal and motivated only up to the point where their confidence in the team's standards and leadership was satisfied. Defense of the country was a serious game, where the outcome was about saving lives instead of scoring points. But Powell was an excellent coach. He became known as someone who assumed the best, rather than the worst, of those under him. And he tended to give his staff rewards to live up to instead of punishments to live down.

According to Weinberger, Powell "prepared papers, planned all trips, had the staff organized, and knew all the people to call." Weinberger believed Powell knew "all of the buttons to push."[2] Powell was a team player and worked especially well with Weinberger. In the space of two years, the two traveled to thirty-five countries. Anywhere that Weinberger went, wrote Simeon Booker in *Ebony* magazine in 1988, Powell also appeared as a kind of "junior Secretary of Defense."[3]

Booker wrote that although Powell was "less of a public person" than Weinberger, he was "very effective within the system." The bickering and immobility that characterized the relationship between the staffs of Weinberger's Defense and George Shultz's State departments disappeared. The two departments disagreed over arms negotiations, with State wanting to speed up arms reduction talks faster than Defense. Through Powell's firm yet subtle brokering, the public friction disappeared. He was at his desk at 6:30 A.M., thoroughly professional and unflappable, not only able to grasp the major policy issues but to detect "dissonance (as distinguished from sound policy)." In a "low-key, unobtrusive manner,"[4] he chaired executive meetings and managed the daily budget reports of the Pentagon's trillion-dollar weapons program. He seldom left his office before 7:00 P.M.

If the occasion demanded it, said Booker, Powell could be a "tough-as-nails military man who has little patience for flabby reasoning."[5] Yet he had "compassion and soul."[6]

As a political realist, Powell was willing to question the military odds of success of U.S. arms support for Nicaragua's contras, a success promised in President Ronald Reagan's right-wing campaign policy. Powell had been the principal administration supporter of the face-saving compromise that continued humanitarian aid to the contras while ending all military aid. Powell made no secret that he considered the contras—whom Reagan had described in terms making them seem the moral equivalent of the Founding Fathers—a waste of tax money.

On Nicaragua and Panama, Powell opposed Elliot Abrams, the assistant secretary of state for inter-American affairs, who strongly supported the contras and military intervention against Noriega. But Powell was not and had never been a boat rocker. While willing to express his opinions when asked, he rarely promoted initiatives on his own.

At the Defense Department, Powell became involved in a plan to deliver missiles to Iran. Because of the United States' poor relationship with Iran, such a plan was fraught with political risks and potentially illegal. Powell warned Weinberger of the danger of not notifying Congress and also sent a memo to the national security adviser and his key assistants reminding them of the legal requirement to notify Congress of the arms transfer. As it turned out, they ignored Powell's memo.

In June 1986, Powell left the Pentagon for military duty and got what had been another longtime dream: an infantry command of nearly 100,000 troops, or what is considered a full army, the crack V Corps in Frankfurt, West Germany. In the normal course of increasing rank and military responsibility, he should first have taken command of a division-size unit of 20,000 soldiers. But his superiors felt that Powell's demonstrated ability at the Pentagon proved beyond doubt his ability to command a full army. He later said that when he was commanding general of V Corps, he was "probably the happiest general in the world."[7]

A month after receiving this assignment, Powell received another star—his second—making him a lieutenant general. He was forty-nine years old.

In November of that year the risks of the missile plan became apparent as revelations were made public that the national security adviser, his chief deputy, and many others had attempted to raise money to finance so-called rebels seeking to overthrow the pro-Soviet, albeit legitimate, government in Nicaragua.

Such a deal, from any number of points of view, was illegal. By the end of that month, the Iran-contra scandal, as the ill-fated plan was known, had cost the national security adviser, Rear Admiral John Poindexter, and his deputy, Lieutenant Colonel Oliver North, their jobs.

At the end of November, Frank Carlucci was appointed assistant to the president for national security affairs, usually known as the national security adviser. One of the first things Carlucci did was to call Powell in Frankfurt to be his deputy. The administration needed Powell, he said. Powell refused outright to give up his military command. Carlucci called Powell in Frankfurt again and again, pleading for Powell to come back to Washington and serve as Carlucci's deputy.

"No way," said Powell.[8]

On the third call, Carlucci sounded so desperate that Powell rang him back to reassure his former boss that there was nothing personal about his refusal. Candidly, Powell then explained his real reservation.

"Frank," he said, "you should know I've been questioned about Iran-Contra because of those Tow missiles and may be asked to testify. That could be a problem."[9]

"Colin," Carlucci said, "I've talked to everybody. You're clean. I wouldn't ask you to give up this command if I didn't need you. The Commander in Chief needs you."[10]

"If he really wants me," Powell said, "then I have to do it."[11]

The next night, Powell's home phone rang in what he thought was a higher-than-normal pitch, a signal White House operators use when calling. When Powell picked up the phone, he heard a familiar voice. It belonged to President Reagan.

"I know you've been looking forward to this command," Reagan said, referring to Frankfurt, "but we need you here."[12]

"Mr. President," Powell responded, "I'm a soldier, and if I can help, I'll come."[13] His new assignment: deputy assistant to the president for national security affairs, or deputy national security adviser. This meant that Powell would advise the national security adviser as well as advise the president directly on when to use military force and on the costs and consequences of military action. Powell's command of the V Corps had lasted only six months.

During the various Iran-contra investigations, Powell became known as "the honest broker" for his actions, as someone who did not "go above the law." Weinberger said, "His whole conduct during that time was impeccable. He was the first one who started catching these very strange intelligence reports that made references to things we didn't know anything about," said Weinberger, referring to the dealings with Iran. "He brought them in to me, and I said I wanted to know a great deal more about it."[14]

Weinberger and Powell had opposed trading arms with Iran, claimed Weinberger. "He and I discussed it many times. When the final decision was made we saw it through with the greatest possible reluctance and did what we were, in essence, ordered to do."[15]

As details of the Iran-contra affair became public, there were congressional investigations and hearings, and lawsuits were brought against many former Reagan advisers. With Carlucci, Powell reorganized the National Security Council according to the recommendations of Senator John Tower's investigative commission. The National Security Council (NSC), by statutory requirement, is headed by the president and is also composed of the vice-president, the secretary of state, and the secretary of defense. The council is advised by the director of the Central Intelligence Agency (representing that particular intelligence community) and the chairman of the Joint Chiefs of Staff (representing the military establishment). Other people often participate in NSC meetings, such as the national security adviser—NSA—who may, depending on the president's time, act as a go-between from the president to the rest of the council. The NSA is usually more of a coordinator and adviser than policy maker, but in various administrations the NSA has also set policy. Sometimes, as in the case of Henry Kissinger during the Nixon administration, the NSA has actually been more influential and powerful than the cabinet members.

At times, too, NSC members have competed with each other for influence or treaded on each other's toes, causing dissonance in administration foreign policy. Such had been the case during the Reagan administration when George Shultz was secretary of state and Caspar Weinberger was secretary of defense. In the case of the Iran-contra scandal, the NSA staff had either secretly carried out the wishes of the president or acted of its own accord. Whatever the source of its directives, the disarray in the NSA's office was a source of embarrassment to the Reagan administration and required a strong hand to tidy up the mess.

And a good thing that the strong hand came along when it did, for just as the Reagan presidency seemed paralyzed by the scandal, Soviet Premier Mikhail Gorbachev was impatiently seeking an end to the arms race. Carlucci and Powell saved the day for the Reagan administration. While Carlucci ran interference within the upper levels of cabinet officials and Congress, Powell took charge of the National Security Council, rebuilt the staff, and coordinated the work of the Pentagon, the State Department, and the CIA.

In frequent meetings with the press, Powell showed himself to be adept, frank, and charming—the last quality especially noted by Washington political insiders. The press conferences made Powell seem almost as influential at the White House as Carlucci.

Powell had not been back in Washington long when he and Alma received terrible news. Their son, Michael, then an Army lieutenant in West Germany, had been riding in a jeep when the driver lost control. The vehicle turned over, breaking Michael's pelvis in six places. He required nearly twenty-two pints of blood.

Michael's survival, the Army doctors explained, hung in the balance. And they said that if the young officer survived, he probably would be confined to a wheelchair for the rest of his life. After four days in an intensive care unit, Michael was flown to Walter Reed Army Medical Center in Washington, D.C., for surgery. The operation seemed desperate, without a chance of success, but Powell refused to let Michael give up hope. "You'll make it," he repeated to his son. "You want to make it, so you will make it!"[16]

Michael's surgery proved successful enough for him to move into the Powell home in Fort Myer, Virginia. For weeks he received daily therapy. Throughout the ordeal, the general kept repeating,

"You'll make it." For months, however, Michael struggled for his life and today is still recovering from serious nerve damage.[17]

It was a terrible time for the Powells. Michael's fortitude, however, became an inspiration to his father. None of Powell's wartime injuries matched Michael's fractured hip in severity. One moment Michael was a bright, young first lieutenant looking forward to a military career, and, said Powell, "a minute later he was fighting for his life."[18]

Both Michael's hip injuries and his recovery were painful. While Michael was bedridden, said Powell, he was heavily medicated, so he was not aware of how excruciating the pain was until the medication was stopped "and he realized he had a fight on his hands," as he struggled to learn to walk.[19]

The whole Powell family was supportive during Michael's ordeal, and Powell himself was proud that Michael showed himself to be "a very strong young man." Powell has credited Michael with acting to cure himself, never doubting that he would get over his injuries.[20]

A year and a half after his accident, Michael had recovered enough to walk with a cane. In the succeeding two years, he married his childhood sweetheart, had a son, began attending Georgetown law school, and worked at the Pentagon.

During Michael's recovery, Powell was working his magic in the National Security Council. He charmed the press and influenced the president. Thomas Griscom, the White House communications chief, recalled that Powell successfully argued, over State Department objections, for tough language in a Reagan speech for a June 1987 appearance at the Brandenburg Gate in West Berlin.

"Mr. Gorbachev," Reagan said, "open this gate . . . tear down this wall."[21]

As far as the Reagan administration was concerned, Powell had secured a firm position of trust in the Republican foreign policy establishment, in spite of the fact that no one really seemed to know Powell's party affiliation.

6

★
NATIONAL SECURITY ADVISER
★

IN 1987, CASPAR WEINBERGER RESIGNED AS SECREtary of defense and was replaced by Frank Carlucci. Considering Powell's experience, abilities, and connections, it came as no surprise when on November 5, 1987, President Reagan appointed Colin Powell National Security Adviser, the first black in such a post.

Powell, the "golden boy" in the Reagan administration, was deluged with invitations for speeches, appearances, and offers for honorary degrees. Powell was a rarity among major officials in the Reagan administration: a black who openly supported black aspirations. During his tenure he would continue to make it a point to be accessible to black reporters, often giving them the first crack at a story.[1]

Within days after being appointed as NSA, Powell accepted an invitation to speak to his first black group, the women's auxiliary of the James Reese Europe American Legion post, Washington's oldest black patriotic organization. It was November, and the beginning of winter was still weeks away, but a freak blizzard suddenly brought the nation's capital to a standstill. Powell's administrative staff wanted him to cancel the meeting—especially since the streets were reportedly blocked by snow drifts and the meeting was many blocks away at Howard University. When his secretary called the legion post, she learned that only a dozen women were in attendance. Powell insisted that even those few were too many to disappoint. "No, I have to go," he told his secretary. "You don't understand." So as soon as he ended a White House meeting, he rushed out to his car and cut a track through the snow-filled streets to Howard University.[2]

The trip over the clogged streets took nearly two hours; Powell may have regretted not walking instead. Yet he was rewarded by his effort in the warm response of the legion faithful.

In his speech, Powell revealed his strong identity with black Americans and demonstrated his versatility in speaking with authority on subjects outside of military matters. He briefly reviewed black military progress. Before he could finish his historical summary, the aged widows had tears in their eyes and gave him a standing ovation. In his later comments to the audience, he displayed a remarkable lack of bitterness at the discrimination blacks in the military had suffered. Speaking of his own experiences, Powell said: "When I came along in 1958, I was able to capture all of what was done before by men in segregated units denied the opportunity to advance. They had the potential as I might have had. . . . It's different now, but we still have a long way to go. We should be grateful for what the men and women have done before. We cannot let the torch drop."[3]

Powell's ability to read his audience and respond appropriately was prominently displayed in December 1987, the month Soviet Premier Gorbachev visited the United States to sign a treaty eliminating Intermediate Range Nuclear Forces. Powell, in his position as NSA, arranged the meeting, starting with an opening-day joint Soviet-American breakfast of pancakes, sour cream, and caviar for Vice-President George Bush at the Soviet embassy. Besides managing the meetings of the president and vice-president with Premier Gorbachev, Powell set up the press conferences and briefed reporters on the disagreements of the superpowers regarding the United States' Strategic Defense Initiative, or Star Wars program.

Powell headed the planning of two more Reagan-Gorbachev meetings during 1988. The political value of the meetings might have been disregarded by someone of less political acumen than Powell, or left unexploited by someone with less skill at promotion. But Powell was very ambitious, as much for his own career as for the administration that elevated him. He well knew the intense public concern with peace and defense, just as he knew how important these themes were as political campaign issues. Accordingly, he kept Vice-President Bush informed on the treaty talks. Details from the talks would give Bush an edge over his main rival, Democratic presidential candidate Michael Dukakis.

Powell's briefing of Bush on security issues was not required by law, but it was one way, according to White House communications chief Thomas Griscom, that Powell "took fairly good care of" Bush, to give Bush an edge in debating security issues with Dukakis.[4]

As national security adviser, Powell reported directly to the president, helping the commander-in-chief and the National Security Council achieve U.S. foreign policy and national security goals. Powell's role was to see that the Council functioned as a policy-making unit and as an advisory committee on U.S. strategy. He operated less like the training coach of a football team, such as he had been in various military commands, and more like the head coach who schedules games, sets the calendar of the team's games, and explains the game to the manager or owner. Powell arranged for the members of the Council and the Council's advisers to have access to classified military, economic, and politically sensitive information, in order for them to be able to advise the president. Powell collected and analyzed information and then assembled it in a form comprehensible and less time-consuming to the president. According to Powell, "the NSC system was set up so the President would get the benefit of a systematic process of advice and deliberation before making a decision. The integrity of that process [was] my responsibility."[5]

Powell briefed the president on key issues like defense and international economics and provided him only with serious ideas on the subjects. He prevented what he called "pet rocks," "dumb ideas," and crackpot suggestions—ideas without substance—from distracting the president. When no one on the staff or in the cabinet could adequately resolve a problem, then it went before the president. "By the time issues in contention reach[ed] the NSC for presentation to the President," he said, "the easy answers [were] usually all gone."[6]

By then, of course, Powell and his staff had researched the problem from every angle, soliciting the knowledge and opinions of experts in the Central Intelligence Agency, military, FBI, State Department, foreign intelligence agencies, and universities. Powell saw to it that every bit of pertinent information was presented to the president so that he could make an informed decision on an issue. Only when Powell had exhausted all sources did he sleep well at night, regardless of whose toes he had stepped on—and usually he had stepped on someone's toes. For example, in the arms reduction talks with the Soviet Union during the final days of the Reagan administration, Powell frequently mediated disputes between Secretary of State George Shultz, who felt that the president was foot-dragging on arms control, and Secretary of Defense Frank Carlucci, who wanted to move more slowly. At one meeting, as tempers flared between Carlucci and Shultz, Powell interrupted them and said, "George, some of your people want to give away the store. The President isn't going to do it."[7]

He then turned to Carlucci. "If we listened to some military men," Powell told him, "there would never be a step toward peace."[8] Powell informed both men that he expressed the opinion of the president himself. Powell claimed that no matter whom he had offended, so long as he had given his superiors the truth, his conscience was clean and he slept "like a baby."[9]

Powell had to be absolutely impartial with the cabinet officers, though he might disagree with them. He also had to broker disputes and mediate between strong personalities, which he did successfully. None of the disputes of the kind between a cautious Weinberger and an impatient Secretary of State George Shultz in 1987 over arms reduction talks with the Soviets erupted while Powell was NSA. Powell himself kept a low profile, his aim being "to help make policy, not headlines."[10]

He also successfully reduced friction between the secretary of state and the NSC, something very much apparent in the past. The one thing he wasn't, he said, was "another foreign minister or competitor to the Secretary of State." Powell's aim was "to help him [the secretary of state] do his job, and he and I both have the same job, and that's to push forward the foreign policy of the President. We're here to support the President in *his* foreign policy."[11]

The virtue of being "personal" adviser to the president meant that Powell could offer honest, or as he once put it, "unvarnished," views, without fear of tailoring his opinions to suit some other superior's point of view. The president's well-being was Powell's only consideration.[12]

Powell's philosophy was that during a crisis, "any President" would "want support from his own staff to help him sort out differing views from his Cabinet officials . . . to see that his decisions, once made," would be "carried out as he intended."[13] Powell won the trust of the president enough to perform sensitive and unreported missions to foreign governments in Angola and the Horn of Africa. He also conducted investigations into government agencies when the president wished to keep the report confidential even from his personal staff.

As a West Wing official—so called because of the location of his office at the White House—Powell found himself forever publicly exposed. He had to be always prepared to issue a statement that could alter international relations. Powell had to have a "helluva lot of information" to know when to speak and when to issue a "No comment!" to a reporter's question. Releasing confidential material, erroneous information, or deliberate lies to the public could produce headlines damaging to the president.[14]

To Powell, information was the "lifeblood" of the NSA: "If you're not on top of the information system, you're not dealing with the lifeblood of the organization."[15] He did not mind the enormous amount of detailed reading and note taking he had to perform daily. The NSA had to have information that was as complete and accurate as possible. Powell had to know the full story about every policy issue or piece of information that might have an effect on the United States. To that end he often did much of the legwork in checking, sometimes directly confronting a source to see if the person actually meant one thing and not another. Sometimes Powell's hands-on method was hard on his staff; they never knew how much detail he wanted on a given topic. On the other hand, Powell's voracious appetite for facts encouraged staff diligence in gathering accurate information.

In 1988, the NSC staff organized numerous defense summit meetings with NATO and economic summits with the major industrial democracies. Powell also provided the president with information on the free trade agreement with Canada, the Intermediate Range Nuclear Forces Treaty, the Persian Gulf, and defense spending. Powell also kept informed on the explosive situations in Haiti and the Philippines, both of which had experienced major revolutions.

Regional hot spots causing concern to the administration were in the immediate "backyard," so to speak, of the United States—namely, Nicaragua and Panama. Powell thought the United States should support the Guatemala peace accords, a Nicaraguan peace plan drawn up by Latin American leaders, and he didn't think much of the contras, the U.S.-backed right-wing rebels in Nicaragua.

At the same time, Powell insisted that the United States had a stake in the security and independence of countries on the borders of the Soviet Union, particularly Afghanistan, a country the NSC watched carefully. Powell became an advocate of covert aid to the Moslem rebels fighting Soviet occupation in Afghanistan.

Another place that drew Powell's attention in 1988 was South Africa, where blacks had been stripped of all citizenship rights for nearly a half-century. Powell saw to it that America's vital interests in South Africa's strategic minerals (minerals that the United States could obtain nowhere else for its jet planes and tanks) and the protection of the sea lanes to the Indian Ocean around the Cape of Good Hope were balanced by the desire of an administration to end apartheid peacefully.

In 1988, he told reporter James Blount of *about . . . time* magazine, "We continued to watch the situation in Southern Africa . . . and the President's personal commitment had to do with removing the system of apartheid. There's a lot of vague disagreement as to the best tactics for doing that, but there's no question about the President's commitment. . . . It is clearer now than ever that apartheid is doomed. Change *will* come to South Africa." Within two years, racist Prime Minister P. W. Botha had been replaced by moderate reformer F. W. de Klerk, who released black leader Nelson Mandela, started negotiating with black groups on a new constitution, and began dismantling the most oppressive features of apartheid. Powell could take a large degree of credit for changing both South African and American administrative thinking on the need for a swift end to apartheid, although most of his work was quietly persuasive and out of public view.[16]

Most Americans probably were unaware in

1988 that Powell had become a principal architect of American defense strategy in Europe. Powell, who worked closely with Caspar Weinberger to shift some of the defense burden of Europe to European countries, told Blount that "ninety percent of the ground forces of Europe are not U.S. forces, they're European forces. They contribute the lion's share of the manpower and the lion's share of the combat power to the alliance now. We are encouraging them to do more. They did a lot more from the late 1960s until the late 1970s when we were quite occupied in Vietnam."[17]

Arguing that it was in the best interest of both the United States and the Soviet Union not to undermine NATO's strategy of flexible response, Powell foresaw that not all crises in Europe might require a nuclear response from the United States. And as Europe took over American military roles in defense, he said that NATO would still have a secure nuclear and conventional deterrent force, with ground-based nuclear systems supplemented by aircraft, tanks, and submarines.

Despite his work for peace, Powell was against any set of negotiations leading to complete disarmament of the superpowers. "It's armaments," he told Blount, "that has kept us strong, and it's armament that's kept peace on the earth for the last forty years."[18]

Using the same reasoning—that a strong defense deters aggression and makes for a lasting peace—he opposed removing nuclear forces from Europe. When he was corps commander in Europe, he never wanted to be faced with "the free Russian Army" without knowing that he could resort to nuclear weapons if it ever came to that—"God forbid." He believed that the surest guarantee that we would never have to resort to nuclear weapons was to view nuclear weapons as "a deterrence to war."[19]

In 1988, U.S. foreign policy had as a guiding principle the "centrality of democracy. Democratic accountability in our own policy-making; human rights in the Communist world; democracy in Central America; a democratic future for South Africa."[20]

But on the anniversary of Martin Luther King, Jr.'s birthday in 1989, Powell wrote, "Although the military was light-years ahead of any institution in our society in equal rights and equal opportunity, it nevertheless was part of a society with an unfulfilled dream."[21] Powell had not forgotten the need for democracy at home.

7

Next Stop: The Pentagon

During the 1988 election campaign, Republican candidate George Bush wanted to appear familiar with the intricacies of U.S.-Soviet arms negotiation and show that he could handle Soviet leaders, so he turned once again to National Security Adviser Powell to polish his public image. In addition to briefing the vice-president on arms control negotiations, Powell made sure that Bush attended a widely publicized actual destruction of the first missiles banned by the 1987 treaty that eliminated intermediate range nuclear forces. At the final meeting between President Reagan and Premier Gorbachev on Governors Island, Powell set up the schedule so as to give Bush maximum photo presence standing with Reagan and Gorbachev. It was a masterful manipulation of public relations during the presidential campaign.

Just before the presidential election, Reagan signed an order promoting Powell to a full four-star general, effective April 1989. On the last day in 1988 that President Ronald Reagan conferred with Powell, Powell told Reagan, "The world is quiet today, Mr. President."[1]

In January 1989, President-elect George Bush called Powell and, after thanking and complimenting him for his services to the Reagan administration, said simply, "I think I ought to have my own national security adviser."[2]

Bush's decision caught Powell by surprise and left him feeling dejected. The day he left the NSC, Powell said he "went home to watch the inauguration on TV. At 1:30 that afternoon, I absentmindedly picked up my White House phone to place a call. It was dead."[3] Standard administrative practice was to change the phone number when personnel changed. The dead phone was a little thing, but it magnified for Powell his disappointment at having lost his job. Powell wondered whether it was time to leave the Army for a more lucrative career.

But what to do next? His experience as national security adviser reinforced his belief that he was "first and foremost a military man." At the NSC, he had vowed over and over that he was "an Army officer even though he appeared in diplomatic costume."[4]

General Carl Vuono, the Army chief of staff, telephoned Powell. "If you want to come home to the Army," Vuono said, "we have a job for you." And a New York literary agent told Powell he could get a million dollars on the lecture circuit.[5]

Powell divided a piece of paper into two columns. Under one column he wrote *Reasons to Stay in the Army* and under the other he wrote *Reasons to Leave the Army*. It was easy for him to write down a dozen reasons to stay, but he could think of only one reason to leave: money.[6]

He still loved military life. And the Army had taken care of his son, Michael, after the jeep accident. Only his youngest daughter, Annmarie (then nineteen) remained in college at William and Mary, from which Michael and their older daughter, Linda, had graduated. Powell talked with his family and friends and decided to stay in the Army. He was appointed head of the Forces Command at Fort McPherson in Atlanta.

In his new post, Powell had to ensure that about one million active duty Army people, reservists, and National Guard members were properly prepared to defend the continental United States and Alaska or to go anywhere that conventional warfare erupted. His budget was over $10 billion.

In early August 1988, President Bush asked Powell to be the next chairman of the Joint Chiefs of Staff, the nation's top military post. All along, Powell's preference had been for a military career over a civilian job. But chairman of the Joint Chiefs was an ideal position for him, given his career sentiments. Being chairman required interaction with the civilian side of government, where Powell could influence policy decisions as well as see that policy was carried out.

Calling Powell the "complete soldier," President Bush said in a ceremony at the Rose Garden on August 11 that Powell would "bring leadership, insight and wisdom to our efforts to keep our military strong and ready." And he added that "it is most important that the chairman . . . be a person of breadth, judgment, experience and total integrity. Colin Powell has all those qualities and more." Bush said Powell had a "truly distinguished military career" and was "a distinguished scholar." The chairman, said Bush, would have a "significant role in determining our military requirements and in developing the defense budget. He is the principal adviser on all military issues to the secretary of defense and to [me]."[7]

Turning to Bush at the end of the ceremony, Powell said, "Mr. President, I am ready to go to it."[8]

In a keynote speech to the fourteenth annual convention of the National Association of Black Journalists on August 17, Powell said that he wanted news reports to say that his "appointment would never have been possible without the sacrifices of those black soldiers who served this great nation in war for nearly three hundred years."[9]

Powell praised the Buffalo Soldiers of the nineteenth century and Teddy Roosevelt's four black regiments who charged up San Juan Hill in Cuba during the Spanish-American War. "We've never seen a picture of them," he said, referring to the black regiments.[10] He added that "almost all barriers have now dropped" in the military but that "there are still more rivers to be crossed."[11]

Powell also praised several outstanding black officers: General Roscoe Robinson, the first black Army four-star general; General Bernard B. Randolph, an Air Force four-star general; and Generals Benjamin Davis, Sr. and Jr., whose achievements made possible his own. As Powell noted, he rose so high today only because of those black military giants. "The real story," he said, "is that, yes, I climbed and I climbed well and I climbed hard. . . . I climbed over . . . the backs and the contributions of those who went before me."[12]

Citing himself as a lesson, Powell said that young people "have got to prepare themselves. They have got to be ready. . . . But now that I am on top of that cliff looking ahead, there are still some more hurdles to be crossed and our young people have to be ready." The achievements of blacks in the military, he said, showed that there is great opportunity for young people who prepare themselves, and he regretted that such opportunity was less available in civilian society. Nevertheless, he foresaw that discriminatory barriers would fall "so that achievement and recognition [would] be based solely on performance."[13]

But it was the military that was leading the way to greater opportunity for all groups in society. And Powell pointed to the recent appointment of the first woman as corps captain at the U.S. Military Academy as evidence that there is "meritocracy . . . within the armed forces of the United States . . . that regrettably does not exist in every part of our society, even within your own profession [journalism]."[14]

Finally, Powell turned to peace and military power. Quoting poet Langston Hughes, civil rights leader Martin Luther King, Jr., and abolitionist Frederick Douglass—three prominent black Americans—Powell maintained that peace can be accomplished only through military strength. Communism, he said, was failing around the world. The Marxists "know their system is broken. They know it cannot meet the challenges of the twenty-first century."[15]

The absence of conflict, Powell concluded, favored the United States' economic system. Quoting King, Powell added: "Freedom has always been an expensive thing."[16]

When the Atlanta Chamber of Commerce honored Powell with a farewell dinner at Fort McPherson, they gave him a citation stating that his length of service, while being "the shortest," cast yet "the longest shadow."[17]

Powell's appointment to chairman of the Joint Chiefs of Staff was special for reasons other than his race. For one thing, a number of generals more senior in rank than Powell were in consideration for the post. For another, Defense Secretary Richard B. Cheney recommended to Bush that Powell serve a double term of four years instead of the customary two-year stint. Previous chairman Admiral William Crowe recommended that Air Force General Robert T. Herres, then vice-chairman of the Joint Chiefs, succeed him for a two-year term, so as to give Powell additional command experience. But Cheney passed over fifteen more senior generals, in addition to bypassing Herres, to appoint Powell.

"Bob was the other choice," Cheney said of

Herres in an interview with *The Washington Post*. "It boiled down to those two basically. I did not like the idea of going for two years" with one chairman and then switching to another. "My judgment was that you ought to go for the best you could get as soon as you could get him."[18]

The country's military chain of command descends from the president to the secretary of defense. Directly below the secretary is the chairman of the Joint Chiefs of Staff; the other chiefs of staff are composed of the heads of the Army, Navy, Air Force, and Marines. The chain of command then runs directly from the chairman to the chiefs. The defense secretary manages the Pentagon's one million civilian employees, while the chairman of the Joint Chiefs oversees the 2.1 million active-duty men and women in the armed forces. When the president or defense secretary needs military advice or wishes to give orders to the military, he goes through the chairman, whether the command is to set a budget, reduce the forces, or mobilize the troops for war. It is up to the chairman to ensure that the military faithfully and successfully achieves the mission set by the president.

Since 1986, the position of the chairman of the Joint Chiefs of Staff has become more than that of a glorified messenger boy for the Army, Navy, Air Force, and Marines. The Goldwater-Nichols Reorganization Act of 1986 elevated the status, authority, and power of the office of chairman over the offices of other service chiefs, added a vice-chairman, and enlarged the chairman's office staff.

With new authority, the position of chairman has gained new political stature. "Goldwater-Nichols," says Lawrence Korb, director of public policy education at the Brookings Institution, "changed the Pentagon like nothing else in recent memory."[19]

Many groups were pleased with Powell's selection as the nation's top soldier, but none so visibly as African-Americans. It offered a positive counterweight to sensational press reports about problems with poor blacks. It gave the press a new focus on blacks. Blacks themselves were pleased that a black military officer would emerge as the top policy maker, higher in rank and power than any other black in American history.

"The general," said Spann Watson, a retired Air Force fighter pilot who promotes greater public awareness of the contributions of blacks in the military, "represents a new era, a new atmosphere, and a new breed. His confirmation could be the turning point in Black America to adopt new strategies."[20]

In the black press there was open speculation about how the general could be "effective in conversations with President Bush on a lot more subjects than military affairs."[21] Initial reports boasted that Powell strove "to reach his people" in a speech to a Southern Christian Leadership Conference convention where Powell underscored the need for "reclaiming hopeless young Black lives."[22]

The Powell family's official residence was now Quarters 6, the chairman's official home overlooking Grant Avenue. Powell's new office was a large room in the E-Ring, the outermost corridor of the Pentagon. He had a picture-window view of the Potomac river. On the floor he installed a thick dark blue carpet. To the side of his work table, he placed an antique chair, couch, and matching chair upholstered in a maroon-colored cloth. Over the couch he hung *Chasing the Victorio,* by Larry Wilkerson, a painting of Lt. Henry O. Flipper (class of 1877), the first black graduate of West Point.

According to Powell, "That young lieutenant was the first black graduate of West Point in 1877. He was cashiered out of the Army on false charges because he was black. He went on to a distinguished career in public life [as a civil engineer]. They reinstalled him in the Army honorably eighty years later."[23]

The wall behind Powell's work desk he lined with awards, plaques, commemorative citations and mugs, and an antique shotgun, a gift from former Soviet leader Mikhail Gorbachev. On another award-laden shelf he put a menorah—a seven-branched candelabra that is a symbol of Judaism—given him by an Israeli friend.

Beneath a glass cover on his desk Powell put a quote from the Athenian historian Thucydides: "Of all manifestations of power, restraint impresses men most."[24] He also displayed on his desk a list of rules he had formulated for daily guidance:

COLIN POWELL'S RULES

1. It ain't as bad as you think. It will look better in the morning.

2. Get mad, then get over it.
3. Avoid having your ego so close to your position that when your position falls, your ego goes with it.
4. It can be done!
5. Be careful what you choose. You may get it.
6. Don't let adverse facts stand in the way of a good decision.
7. You can't make someone else's choices. You shouldn't let someone else make yours.
8. Check small things.
9. Share credit.
10. Remain calm. Be kind.
11. Have a vision. Be demanding.
12. Don't take counsel of your fears or naysayers.
13. Perpetual optimism is a force multiplier.

These rules would come in very handy over the next few weeks, since one of the first things on Powell's agenda was a crisis in Panama.

8

★
Just Cause in Panama
★

In 1903, the United States supported a rebel movement in northern Colombia's Central American territory to create a new country called Panama. In exchange, the United States had gotten the rebels to give it a ten-mile-wide strip across the isthmus—the Canal Zone—and virtual control of Panama's affairs. In 1977, the United States relinquished sovereignty over the Panama Canal and agreed to let the Panamanian government assume control over the Canal Zone on December 31, 1999. Despite the agreement, the Panamanians were unhappy with the continued U.S. control of the Canal. Since 1981, Manuel Noriega had exploited U.S.-Panamanian tensions to secure his power. Yet when he claimed to be a friend of the United States and an opponent of anti-U.S. elements, he won U.S. support.

In 1986, the relationship began to sour openly when reports showed that Noriega was involved in drug trafficking and had murdered an opposition leader. In 1987, he was indicted in the United States for drug smuggling and fired as army chief of staff by Panamanian President Eric Arturo Delvalle. Noriega then forced the National Assembly to replace Delvalle, over U.S. protests and sanctions, with another leader.

A former Defense Department official reiterated the long-held Pentagon view that Noriega was "not worth one U.S. soldier's life."[1]

Evidence of Noriega's suspected ties to Colombian druglords and to other criminal activities convinced the Reagan and Bush administrations that the United States had to remove him from power, even if it meant using force.

When Powell was national security adviser, he had apparently favored pardoning Noriega to avoid a military conflict in Panama. His feelings did not change when he was nominated chairman of the Joint Chiefs of Staff.

A nonviolent solution to an increasingly embarrassing situation seemed a good way, too, to avoid diplomatic problems. Powell bore the memories of recent U.S. military disasters such as Desert One, President Carter's 1980 attempted helicopter rescue of American hostages in Iran; the United States' humiliating 1983 withdrawal from Lebanon after a car bomb attack on a marine barracks; and the strong resistance of a handful of Cuban soldiers and workers against a division of American forces in the early days of the Grenada invasion. But it was the defeat in Vietnam that had left U.S. military leadership deeply suspicious of civilian "hawks" who rushed into war without considering the domestic political consequences.

A deal was then discussed in the NSC whereby Noriega would go into exile "peacefully." But on May 10, 1987, television viewers around the world were horrified by scenes of Noriega supporters, with clubs and knives, beating newly elected vice-president Guillermo "Billy" Ford until his white shirt was drenched with blood. For the next two years, Noriega remained a problem without a solution.

The Senate unanimously confirmed Powell as chairman by a rare voice vote on September 9. The news of a coup attempt in Panama on October 1, 1989, two days before Powell's swearing-in as chairman, reminded Powell of his tenure as President Reagan's national security adviser. The coup was reported in American news reports, but there were no signs the rebels were succeeding. Powell was still reluctant to use military force: "By nature, I'm very cautious about the use of the armed forces . . . putting lives on the line. But when it's clear we're going to use them, well, let's use them."[2] In his view, any hastily organized effort was a long shot. The Panamanian rebels needed time to organize effectively.

Powell took the oath of office on October 3 from his immediate boss, Defense Secretary Richard Cheney. Alma Powell held the Bible on which Colin pledged allegiance to the Constitution. Powell was the twelfth chairman of the Joint Chiefs of Staff.

The brass bands, the speeches, and the review of the Army's costumed revolutionary old guard did not deter an aide standing near Powell from answering a cellular telephone. No sooner had Powell completed the oath of office than the aide whispered in Powell's ear. Silently, the chairman listened as the aide described the desperate conditions of anti-Noriega rebel military officers in Panama. The aide told Powell that Noriega was still firmly in power.

As Powell expected, the quick coup attempt against Noriega was suppressed in the next few hours. Many of the Panamanian plot organizers were tricked into disarming themselves by a Noriega promise of amnesty. As soon as they dropped their weapons, they were executed on the spot. Coup leaders in hiding appealed to President Bush: they wanted the United States to militarily intervene to save the captured rebels. Powell had opposed military intervention all along. But the executed Panamanian military officers, whose families personally knew Powell and Bush, now added an urgency to the political need to deal with Noriega once and for all.

In the afternoon of his confirmation day, Powell gave his inaugural address at the Pentagon. There was a large crowd of Pentagon employees on the parade ground overlooking the Potomac. The crowd cheered when Powell reviewed the ceremonial troops. After Cheney introduced Powell, to further cheers, the new chairman addressed the crowd.

To illustrate what he believed the purpose of the military in a democratic society ought to be, he described a painting of a church in a Pentagon stairwell. In the painting, a single family kneels alone at the altar rail—a mother, a young son, a daughter, and a father in uniform, praying together before the father goes off to war. The family is illuminated by sunlight streaming down on them through a stained-glass window.

Powell said the painting made him silently pray for the men and women who served the nation in times of danger. Powell quoted an inscription from the prophet Isaiah underneath the painting: "And the Lord God asked: 'Whom shall I send? Who will go for us?' And the reply came back: 'Here am I, send me.' " The nation, added Powell, had a historic opportunity for creating peaceful change in countries such as Panama under military dictatorships. If the United States was to promote democracy, it needed a ready and strong military that would deter aggression and encourage peace. With the demise of the Soviet power in Central America, the United States was now in a position to help establish democracies there.

"And if we are successful," he concluded, "the men and women of our armed forces will pay only the price of eternal readiness, and not the tragic and precious price of life."[3]

In the week after the failed coup, the president wanted to apply more pressure, both economic and military, on Noriega. As a Vietnam veteran, Powell knew that it would be imprudent for a new chairman to recommend military intervention without either public support or sufficient military preparation to win.

According to one White House official, there

were subtle signs within the White House that Bush had decided on military intervention. But the outside world had no such clues. A week after the failed coup, however, Powell secretly drew up a military contingency plan. The timing of the plan was approved by Bush on October 16 during a meeting in the Oval Office. The scope of the planned invasion, in men and materiel, would make it the largest invasion since the Vietnam War. Powell found the Pentagon eager to use the opportunity to test new technologies of war, like the radar-evading Stealth jet fighter and new methods of combat coordination of land and air units.

On December 15, Noriega had the National Assembly declare him Panama's "maximum leader" and, in an act of extreme provocation, ratify a "state of war" with the United States.

Noriega then provided a prime political motivation for the United States to invade. His forces, in widely publicized events December 16 and 17, killed a Marine officer and abused an American serviceman's wife.

When Powell met with his staff on December 17 he told them that "Noriega has gone over the line." In Powell's words, "everyone sat up straight."[4] Powell took the position that the killing of the Marine was an insult to U.S. honor and that Noriega's declaration of war was an outrage demanding action.

What followed were a series of marathon planning sessions. Finally, an invasion plan was approved that included dropping U.S. reinforcements at two heavily defended locations where U.S. intelligence agencies believed Noriega was likely to be early Wednesday morning. Powell persuaded Cheney to use a larger contingent of troops—crack paratroopers and other specially trained forces—than had been envisioned under earlier invasion plans.

Operation Just Cause, the Pentagon's code name for the invasion, aimed to crush the Noriega regime, arrest Noriega for trial in the United States on drug smuggling charges, and restore the democratically elected government that Noriega had thrown out.

Early on December 19, Powell informed Army Colonel William Smullen III, Powell's aide, that U.S. forces were going to invade Panama. But Powell added that he "wanted to maintain as much normalcy as possible."[5]

Powell's day in fact turned out to be quite normal. He had lost a bet with Naval Academy midshipman Tom Daily over the Army-Navy football game. Since he owed Daily a lunch at the Pentagon, the day before the invasion he met with the midshipman for forty-five minutes and paid for the lunch as promised.

In the afternoon Powell met with Tiffani Starks, the teenage daughter of an Air Force lieutenant colonel. The colonel was a friend of the Powells, and Tiffani wanted to interview Powell for a high school writing assignment on famous people. Despite his busy schedule, Powell greeted Tiffani and her father in his office and for nearly fifteen minutes—

the meeting had been scheduled for five minutes—held them spellbound with anecdotes of his career as a soldier.

For the next few hours Powell briefed the White House on last-minute changes in the invasion plan. At 5 P.M. he consulted with the Joint Chiefs and Cheney on avoiding news leaks. Network news programs reported throughout the afternoon that 82nd Airborne paratrooper units and C-141 Starlifter transports were en route to Panama. But none of the programs exposed the military purpose of the unusual troop movements.

Leaving his staff to continue final preparations for the assault, Powell dined with Alma at their residence at Grant Avenue, a roomy, comfortable house full of pink, yellow, and blue pastels. She knew that because a crisis plan would be top secret, she could not know what occupied him. She also knew that he followed a practice—which she supported—of not discussing his work with her.

"There are some things," she said in a 1991 interview for *Ebony* magazine, "you don't talk to him about" at moments of crisis. "I wouldn't go to him . . . to say the car's not running or the bathroom needs a new plunger. Nor would he be interested, except on the surface, in some little story about what the children are doing."[6]

Alma did not question him that evening when he told her that he was returning to the Pentagon. She knew that his job required unexpected absences for long periods of time. Powell took a nap in his office, and at 11:52 P.M. he entered the crisis room.

Within the next hour, Guillermo Endara was secretly sworn in as Panama's president. Just after 12:45 A.M., Powell ordered General Thurman to commence the assault with 26,000 troops and to arrest Noriega.

At 1:40 A.M. President Bush's press secretary, Marlin Fitzwater, interrupted regular television programming to announce the invasion to the American public. Fitzwater stated that the aims of the operation were to restore a democratic government to Panama and to apprehend Noriega. Six hours later President Bush appeared on the screen to explain why the military operation was necessary. "I took this action," said Bush, "only after reaching the conclusion that every other avenue was closed."[7]

When Bush left the air, Powell and Cheney appeared live from the Pentagon briefing room to give details of the operation's progress. Powell had spent all night and early morning at the Pentagon but showed no signs of fatigue in the briefing room. He stepped to the podium wearing horn-rimmed glasses. Television cameras panned his face while he used a pointer to show where troop movements and battles were occurring. Many Americans learned for the first time during this briefing of Powell's role as the nation's military leader. At fifty-two years old, the black Army general was trim, handsome, tall, and heavyset, and on television he presented an image of utter confidence. Despite his formal bearing and guarded replies, he usually smiled at tough critical questions. When pressed by a reporter to repeat details of the fighting, Powell detailed in measured tones how Thurman's paratroopers achieved surprise in the predawn hours and were routing Noriega's troops. His briefing was altogether intelligent and well-informed. A reporter asked whether Noriega might not "make life miserable for the U.S. forces down there."

Powell said: "I doubt it. No, I don't think, one, it's been some years since General—Mr. Noriega, the fugitive, has been seen in the jungle, living in the jungle, and I'm not sure he would be up to being chased around the countryside by Army Rangers, Special Forces and Light Infantry units of the Joint Operations Training Center.[8]

"We will chase him," vowed Powell, "and we will find him."[9]

In the next few days the fighting spread across Panama. Even the Pentagon joined critics in revising the projected end of hostilities from "three days" to weeks, or "as long as it takes."[10]

Many critics displayed the "Vietnam Syndrome" and predicted a sharp rise in U.S. casualties—a guerrilla campaign lasting years. Contrary to the critics' predictions, however, the bulk of Noriega's forces were quickly dispersed, or offered only token opposition during the initial week of conflict.

Powell stayed in direct contact with Thurman on a daily basis; he asked detailed questions concerning the progress of the operation to capture Noriega. Each day he wanted to know how stiff resistance was from Noriega's paramilitary units, the "Dignity Battalions," and what were the casualties, both military and civilian. Such direct and frequent contact enabled Powell to call CIA director William Webster and report the freeing of a CIA hostage from a Panama jail. But the American military command was left frustrated and red-faced for four days in the hunt for Noriega.

To the surprise of many observers, reports from occupied parts of Panama City showed that Panamanians welcomed the overthrow of Noriega. Nonetheless the operation was a unilateral one, and the United States had not taken the precaution of consulting with members of the Organization of American States. Many Latin American leaders protested that the invasion was nothing more than Yankee domination. Certainly, the behavior at times of undisciplined American troops gave credibility to the Latin protests.

While Noriega was in hiding, aggressive U.S. troops tried to use martial law to justify destroying the offices of his political supporters. In two widely publicized incidents, the troops violated diplomatic protocol, which safeguards foreign diplomats and embassies from martial laws. Powell ordered Thurman to crack down on troops responsible for reckless tactics.[11]

On Christmas Eve, the dictator revealed that he was hiding under cover of diplomatic immunity at the office of the Vatican representative in Panama City. A few days later, Noriega surrendered to U.S. troops and was soon in chains in a federal prison. Operation Just Cause had been accomplished.

On January 4, Powell went to Panama. He wanted to plan bringing U.S. troops home. The trip showed considerable bravery on his part. Noriega's forces had not all surrendered; some of the ones at large continued to shoot at American troops. But Powell wished to observe the field of battle directly. He wanted to be a hands-on leader.

In just eighty-one days as chairman, Powell had helped to oust Noriega from power in Panama, reversing two years of often strong opposition by senior military officers to the use of U.S. military forces. For his leadership in the Panama crisis, Powell won the country's admiration. Instantly, he became a pop figure in the media. He had led the nation's first major victory in battle since Vietnam. He had demonstrated superb political timing with an overwhelming and swift defeat of Noriega, before domestic antiwar opposition could develop. Above all, he had achieved victory with minimum American casualties. *The Wall Street Journal* headlined one story "Powell Was Perfectly Cast to Plan and Explain Assault."[12]

Had the headline been an epitaph, it would have marked the high point of a military career that any general would envy. But the best for Powell was yet to come.

9

OPERATION DESERT SHIELD

At the beginning of 1990, Noriega sat in a U.S. jail and Communist governments in Eastern Europe and the Soviet Union that were once a threat to the West, teetered on the brink of economic, social, and political collapse. South African and Central American conflicts no longer endangered world peace. In Powell's view, the end of the Cold War and the decline of the Communist superpower meant the Pentagon faced newly ambiguous military dangers requiring political as well as military responses. Good soldiers needed to know when, as well as when not, to fight. "There's no other uses for the military," Powell had said in a 1989 interview, "except for political purposes. We don't exist in a vacuum, we don't use the military for military purposes. We use the military to achieve a political purpose."[1]

For the first time, a number of high officials began to describe Powell's future in terms of political office—the first black president. In the January 1990 issue of *Forbes*, former Secretary of Defense Caspar Weinberger wrote effusively of Powell's po-

Colin (right), age seven, his mother, "Arie," and thirteen-year-old sister, Marilyn, share a bench on a summer vacation day, Jamaica, Long Island, 1944. Every summer the Powell children vacationed on Long Island with cousins and extended family members. *(MARILYN BERNS)*

Colin, age eight, and Marilyn, age fourteen, dressed in Sunday best in front of a billboard on Kelly Street, South Bronx, 1945. *(MARILYN BERNS)*

Colin Powell, in the center, with high school friends in Hunts Point, South Bronx, New York, c. 1948. Most of Powell's friends were children of immigrants to New York, and he recalls that everyone in his neighborhood was a minority. *(GENERAL POWELL, DEPARTMENT OF DEFENSE)*

Colin Powell (right) standing beside his mother, "Arie," sister, Marilyn, and father, Luther, at Marilyn's graduation from New York State University at Buffalo, 1952. Colin's parents insisted on a college education for their children. *(GENERAL POWELL, DEPARTMENT OF DEFENSE)*

At City College in New York (CCNY), Colin joined the Reserve Officers Training Program (ROTC) and the elite marching unit, the Pershing Rifles. On his left shoulder is the golden whipped cord of the Pershing Rifles. Colin was attracted by the status of the Pershing Rifles, not least because the uniform impressed many of the coeds at CCNY (c. 1953).
(GENERAL POWELL, DEPARTMENT OF DEFENSE)

While a student at CCNY, Colin spent part of his summers training with his ROTC unit at Fort Bragg, North Carolina, and he served as Commander of the Guard in July 1957. In North Carolina, Colin first encountered legal segregation off the base. (*GENERAL POWELL, DEPARTMENT OF DEFENSE*)

Lieutenant Colonel Powell, a battalion commander in Seoul, Korea, in 1973, was responsible for the lives of 5,000 troops. Powell enjoyed working with troops in the field, and he drove his own jeep. (*GENERAL POWELL, DEPARTMENT OF DEFENSE*)

Major Colin Powell, on his second tour of Vietnam, June 1968–July 1969. Powell won two purple hearts decorations for his courage and heroism under fire in Vietnam. (*General Powell, Department of Defense*)

Lieutenant General Colin Powell (right), the number two man on the National Security Council (NSC), thanking President Ronald Reagan for nominating him to succeed Frank Carlucci as national security adviser and head of the NSC. Powell is shown at a White House ceremony November 5, 1987, for outgoing secretary Caspar Weinberger (at left). *(AP/WIDE WORLD PHOTOS)*

A Powell family photograph at the White House in 1987. From the left stands daughter Annmarie, son, Michael, daughter, Linda, Lieutenant General Colin Powell, and his wife, Alma. The Powells, despite hectic professional lives, maintain a close-knit family life. *(DENNIS BRACK, BLACK STAR)*

President George Bush, center, applauds General Colin Powell, right, during a ceremony in the Rose Garden of the White House, August 10, 1989, naming the fifty-two-year-old four-star general Powell as the youngest ever chairman of the Joint Chiefs of Staff. Powell replaced retiring Admiral

William Crowe, Jr., in the post, to become the first black to serve as the nation's top military officer. Defense Secretary Dick Cheney, at right, and Vice President Dan Quayle, at far left, join in the applause. *(AP/WIDE WORLD PHOTOS)*

Secretary of Defense Dick Cheney (left) administers the oath of office to General Colin L. Powell, USA, chairman, Joint Chiefs of Staff, October 3, 1989, in the Pentagon. General Powell's wife, Alma, holds the Bible. *(HELENE STIKKEL, DEPARTMENT OF DEFENSE)*

December 20, 1989, General Powell, chairman of the Joint Chiefs of Staff, briefs newsmen on the Pentagon's predawn invasion designed to oust General Manuel Noriega. A map of Panama City is in the background. The Panama invasion introduced Powell to many Americans when he appeared on television to explain the invasion. *(AP/WIDE WORLD PHOTOS)*

General Powell (right), chairman of the Joint Chiefs of Staff, congratulating an unidentified officer outside the Commandancia building in Panama City. The officer participated in the assault on the Panamanian Defense Forces headquarters in the successful overthrow of the dictator Noriega. *(AP/WIDE WORLD PHOTOS)*

General Powell, chairman of the Joint Chiefs of Staff, meeting with Armed Forces media, February 2, 1990, in the Pentagon after the successful capture of Panamanian dictator Noriega. *(HELENE STIKKEL, DEPARTMENT OF DEFENSE)*

General Powell posing with West Point graduate Kristin Baker (right), twenty-two, at the U.S. Military Academy graduation ceremony, June 1, 1990, West Point, New York. Powell, who gave the commencement address, reminded the gathering that he and Baker shared a first. He was appointed the first black chairman of the Joint Chiefs, and Baker, a brigade commander, was the first female captain of the corps of cadets. *(AP/WIDE WORLD PHOTOS)*

First Lady Barbara Bush poses with Chairman of the Joint Chiefs of Staff Colin Powell during a White House reception in Washington, September 18, 1990, honoring black appointees to the Bush administration. *(AP/WIDE WORLD PHOTOS)*

General Colin Powell (left), chairman of the Joint Chiefs of Staff, hosts a joint press conference at the Pentagon for his Soviet counterpart, General Mikhail Moiseyev (center), October 5, 1990. A Soviet translator sits beside Moiseyev. Powell early recognized the political instability of the Soviet Union. *(HELENE STEKKEL, DEPARTMENT OF DEFENSE)*

Powell has always been comfortable with a variety of military leaders. From the left, Lieutenant General Heinz Heasler, chief of the general staff, Swiss Armed Forces, exchange honor guard salutes at the Pentagon on October 10, 1990. Heasler was the guest of Joint Chiefs Chairman Powell at the Pentagon River Entrance Parade Field, where an Armed Forces Full Honor Ceremony was held to commemorate the visit. *(WARD, DEPARTMENT OF DEFENSE)*

Always a hands-on manager, Chairman Powell, on the left, surveys a Marine position in Saudi Arabia near the Kuwait border. Marine Corporal Vincent Rivera (right) stands guard and an unidentified soldier stands as lookout on an armored vehicle. During and after Operation Desert Storm, Powell visited Saudi Arabia to ensure the success of the allied action to evict Iraqi dictator Saddam Hussein's troops from Kuwait. *(AP/WIDE WORLD PHOTOS)*

litical prospects, calling him "the quintessential soldier" who had "a remarkable understanding of the great issues of our time, the problems in world affairs and how our government operates."[2]

Speculation on Powell's political future proved premature, however. After the war in Panama, what seemed to require most of Powell's immediate attention was the size of the military budget—something of great concern to politicians, the military, defense contractors, and ordinary citizens alike. President Bush directed Powell to reduce the size and budget of the U.S. military to the level it was at before Vietnam. Acknowledging the need for budget reductions before the Senate Armed Services Committee, Powell requested "a smaller but ready force" with "quality."[3]

On May 31, Powell addressed the West Point graduating class at West Point, New York. Starting out light and cheerful, he recited "plebe knowledge," the numerous commandments governing cadet life. He had spent a few days at the academy while in ROTC, and now he entertained 20,000 family and friends of the graduates by regaling, almost in rap style, the "plebe knowledge" from memory.

Later he gave a degree to 1st Lieutenant Kristin M. Baker, the first female captain of the corps—West Point's highest cadet honor. "They had," he said, "a running joke as she and I were announced on the same day last October; she became First Captain the day I became Chairman of the Joint Chiefs of Staff."[4] Clearly Powell relished the coincidence of the first black chairman awarding honors to the first female leader of a graduating class at the Army's number one military school.

During his address, the general turned to serious matters and called on the new officers to maintain pride, quality, and strength in "an Army that will be smaller" because of the end of the Cold War with the Soviet Union.[5]

"Let the old General Powell worry about the defense budgets, peace dividends and geopolitical trends," he said. "You go and do what West Point second lieutenants have been doing. Lead your soldiers. Keep them fit and hardy, trained and ready. Keep them proud."[6]

The cadets, he continued, lived during a "watershed in our history . . . where the prospect of a world war is no longer a fear, although the world is still troubled. Nevertheless, the prospect of peace is now more than a dream."[7]

He warned against "dismantling our armed forces when danger seems to be gone. We don't have draftees waiting to get out. Everyone in the armed forces today is a volunteer under contract, and you've got to allow us to manage that down to the new level. Let us manage it in a sensible way over the next couple of years."[8]

In a speech to the National Press Club in June 1990, Powell pleaded with Congress not to reduce the defense budget so drastically that the reduction "will force us to start breaking the back of our armed forces."[9]

In the nine months since being named chairman, he said, he had "been reminded again and again . . . that this is still a dangerous world and that you'd better be able to respond if someone challenges your interests."[10]

Inevitably, Powell observed, a smaller U.S. military would also remove a career opportunity for minorities and the poor, for whom military jobs have provided a traditional path of upward mobility. Unfortunately, Powell's vision of a "prospect of peace" remained no more than a hope that would be soon disappointed.

The oil-rich country of Iraq, nearly 10,000 miles away from Washington, D.C., had friendly relations with the United States. In July of 1990, however, its leader, President Saddam Hussein, told the American ambassador to Baghdad that his southern neighbor, Kuwait, an oil-rich shiekdom, was flooding world markets with oil. The increased supply of oil meant a lower price, reducing profits for Iraq. Saddam was furious. Moreover, he claimed that Kuwait was illegally siphoning oil from the Ramallah oil field, a large oil field straddling the frontier between the two countries. The American ambassador, April Glaspie, urged Saddam to seek a negotiated settlement. And, perhaps because she could not imagine Iraq settling the issue any other way than peacefully, she gave no explicit warning against a violent solution.

On August 2, 1990, to the shock and dismay of nearly every country in the world, Saddam's troops invaded Kuwait and set up a puppet government there. By the time reports reached Powell and the

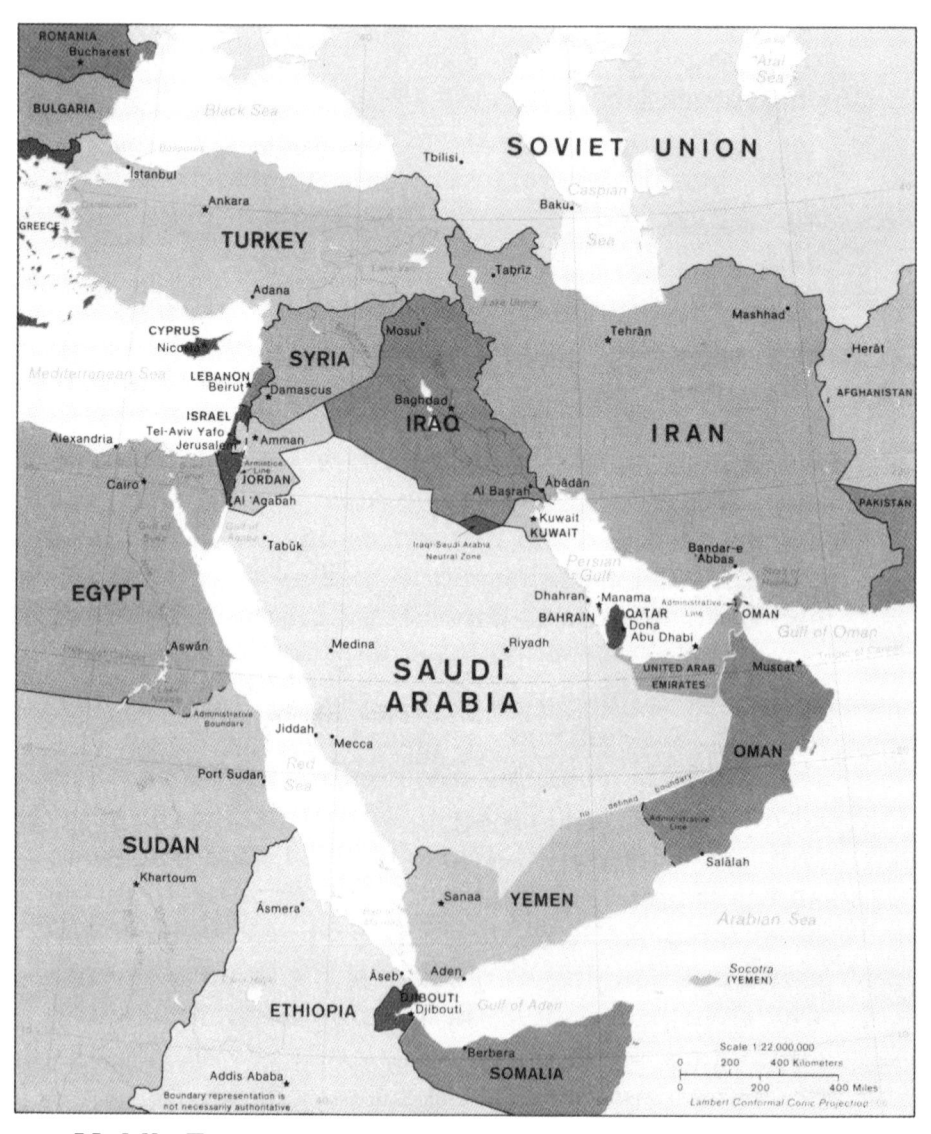

Middle East *(courtesy of the State Department)*

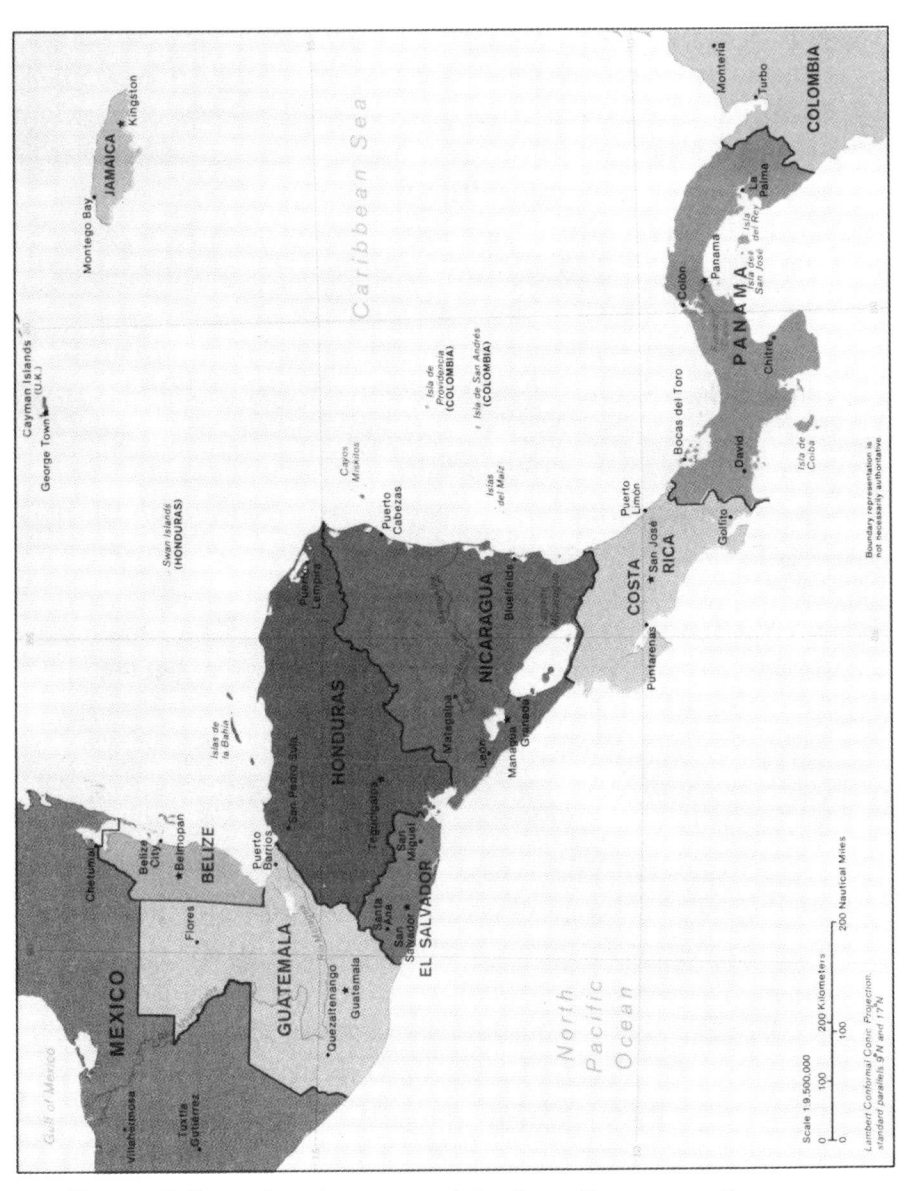

Central America *(courtesy of the State Department)*

White House, Iraqi troops were also deep inside northern Saudi Arabia. More disturbing to Powell, satellite reconnaissance photos of the area showed Iraqi troops consolidating lines of support for a possible conquest of all the countries of the Persian Gulf. If that had happened, Saddam would have controlled most of the world's oil supply and would have been able to dictate the price of world oil.

The record showed Saddam to be a ruthless leader, even though he had served U.S. interests in the Iraqi-Iranian war (1980-88). In his eight-year war with Iran, he had used internationally banned chemical and biological weapons against civilian Iranians and Kurds, a tribal minority scattered among Iraq, Iran, and Turkey. Against his foes within Iraq, his weapons were torture and assassination. He had promised genocide, in a series of luridly explicit addresses, to Israeli Jews. It was common knowledge in diplomatic circles in the Middle East that he was trying to build, or buy, nuclear weapons.

President Bush and Powell were deeply concerned. To them the loss of the oil fields to military aggression and the clear violation of United Nations law—by overthrowing the U.N. member government of Kuwait—made Iraq a clear danger to the interests of the United States and other Western countries. The Reagan administration, ironically, had supported Iraq during its war with Iran (it was supposedly the lesser of two evils) and in fact, the U.S. supported Saddam up to his invasion of Kuwait. Now this "friend" of the United States was turning on its ally. The parallels with Panama were obvious.

Later in the day on August 2, Powell saluted a Marine guard at the White House entrance, marched into the crisis room, and greeted a team of Bush officials waiting for his account of the Iraqi invasion. Drawing on intelligence reports, Pentagon charts, Defense Department analyses, and satellite reconnaissance maps, Powell outlined to President Bush, Defense Secretary Cheney, and the others the magnitude of Iraq's occupation of Kuwait. Powell told them that Iraq's aims seemed to reach further than forcing Kuwait to concede the Ramallah oil field and raising the price of Kuwait's oil.

Powell had strong evidence that Saudi Arabia and the other Gulf states were in danger of Iraqi attack. If persuasion and sanctions, he concluded, failed to get Saddam's troops to withdraw from Kuwait, then nothing short of a U.S. military response would dislodge them or prevent them from taking the entire Gulf. Something had to be done to stop Saddam Hussein, but what?

Powell laid out a contingency plan to defend Saudi Arabia's giant oil fields from Iraqi attack; its code name was Operation Desert Shield. By chance, General H. Norman Schwarzkopf, one of Powell's favorite commanders, had run a computerized war game in July mobilizing 100,000 U.S. troops against Iraqi armored divisions. Powell's modified version of the game plan would involve the fastest large-scale deployment of U.S. forces since World

War II. The next day President Bush ordered Powell to activate the plan.

On August 9, President Bush announced that Iraq would not be permitted to annex Kuwait. "That's not a threat," said the President, "not a boast. That's just the way it's going to be."[11] Bush then decided to send troops to Saudi Arabia to take up "defensive" positions to protect Saudi Arabia and other supposed U.S. interests in the area. He also ordered trade sanctions against Iraq. Other nations followed suit.

In the first week of September, 100,000 American troops were in Saudi Arabia. Operation Desert Shield was no longer a computer game but a reality.

During the early months of the crisis, Powell was at his desk at 6 A.M. in the National Military Command Center, the secret operations post of the Pentagon. He returned there all hours of the day for special briefings. His operations staff meetings were conducted in a large, eavesdrop-proof conference room. Informal meetings with an inner circle of staff took place in his office around a small table with a large telephone console. An adjacent work table was usually littered with maps and reports after he and aides met with a Central Intelligence Agency courier as early as 7:30 A.M.

Moving the troops, weapons, and supplies was more daunting than anything done at the World War II invasion of Normandy. And it all took time. During the month of August, Saddam could have advanced in any direction he chose down the Gulf coast to the Arab emirates, through Jordan and toward Israel. There was nothing to prevent the Iraqis from blowing up the Saudi oil fields.

"You go in with overwhelming force," Powell advised a Senate Armed Services Committee hearing on September 11. "You go in very quickly, and once it's over you get out."[12]

"One of the fondest expressions around," Powell had told one interviewer in August, "is that we can't be the world's policeman. I certainly agree that we should not go around saying we are the world's policeman. But guess who gets called when suddenly someone needs a cop."[13]

Explained Powell, "Iraq is somewhat unique in terms of its ability to threaten and subdue its neighbors, as we have seen with their invasion of Kuwait. I think one of the challenges for us in the future is to make sure that no other small regime accumulates that kind of military power."[14]

On September 19, Powell sat in the second row of Congress for President Bush's speech to a joint session. The president declared that the United States had "drawn a line in the sand" at the Iraq-Kuwait border. The phrase was Powell's contribution to the President's speech, though Powell was not a White House speechwriter. Following the president's address, Powell drove to Andrews Air Force Base, changed into camouflage fatigues, and boarded a giant C-137 plane for a fifteen-hour flight. When he stepped out of the plane, he was in Saudi Arabia. Immediately he drove to visit troops in the desert.

The troops lionized the chairman, treating him

like a star and asking for his autograph. Though Powell still suffered from jet lag, he made a whirlwind tour to the American desert positions, sometimes by helicopter and jeep caravan, but occasionally trekking for short distances in the hot sands. Nearly everywhere, he was "bombarded . . . with questions in front of reporters about when [the troops] would be going home."[15] Powell, much to his regret, could not then answer the question. On this Saudi Arabian trip, Powell learned from a television report that Air Force Chief General Michael Dugan had inadvertently revealed classified information in an interview. Furious as well as saddened by Dugan's leak, Powell set in motion the orders for Dugan's resignation, notwithstanding the personal friendship of the two officers. The Dugan episode underscored Powell's high professional standards. Had Powell violated security and had Dugan been chairman, Powell would have expected the same penalty.

At the end of September, the U.N. Security Council sanctioned a total embargo and blockade on all trade with Iraq. Immediately France, Britain, and twenty-six other countries pledged to send troops to the Gulf in support of a military effort to drive Iraq out of Kuwait. As October began, Powell had 150,000 American troops in Saudi Arabia.

At his desk each morning, Powell began intensively studying top-secret reports on Saddam. Powell learned that despite Saddam's military decorations, the Iraqi had never served in an army and had bestowed the medals on himself without ever directing a battle. That meant Saddam Hussein's power rested on the weakness of his opponents rather than on the strength of his army or on the skill of his commanders.

As bedtime reading, Powell took home a history of Mesopotamia, as Iraq was called in the Bible. The history, he said, took him "back to the period 8000 B.C. in the valleys of the Euphrates and Tigris rivers. It's slowly bringing me up to date."[16]

By October, he had reached 4000 B.C., the point of the invention of the Sumerian language. He intended to reach the present within a week, in order to understand the enemy and the enemy's past. To one reporter who interviewed him then, Powell offered the famous quote from philosopher George Santayana: "Those who do not remember the past are doomed to repeat it." He added, "They are not necessarily doomed to repeat it, but they are not as prepared for the future as they might have been if they had done some historical research.

"Ten or eleven years ago, if you were talking about the Persian Gulf and the Middle East, one of the great fears we had was that it could lead to superpower confrontation. The United States and the Soviet Union could go to war—with each other— and set the stage for World War III. It's almost ludicrous today to think that anything in the Persian Gulf could lead to the United States and the Soviet Union shooting dice over it for real. That's a significant change. And that's exciting."[17]

That October the head of the Soviet Union's General Staff, General Mikhail A. Moiseyev, discussed with Powell in New York City the United Nations' options in the Persian Gulf. "We cannot view the resolution of any crisis like this by means of using arms," said General Moiseyev.[18] The Soviets wanted the U.N. to apply only sanctions against Iraq.

Powell, however, remained adamant in stating the American position: "The United States hopes the situation can be resolved peacefully. We are not eliminating any of the options that are available to the President."[19]

When Powell spoke of the decision to send troops to the Persian Gulf, he displayed a characteristic modesty and deference to the president. "It never became fact," he said to one interviewer, "until the President said 'Go.' But in the structuring of options, it was obvious that I anticipated, as we all did, that it would mean our colleagues going to the Middle East, the young men and women who serve us so well."[20]

From as early as October, Powell had decided that the U.S. would need an imaginative and daring plan if the country was to avoid another protracted Vietnam War. After he obtained the president's and Cheney's approval, he launched his secret "enhanced option." The plan would put a complete offensive-army-size force in Kuwait. Only twenty-five other senior officers were privy to the "option."[21]

By mid-October, more than 200,000 troops were stationed in Saudi Arabia, and an armada of warships was in the Persian Gulf.

Although Powell was preparing for war, he hoped for a peaceful outcome. Like his idol General Dwight D. Eisenhower, Powell was suspicious of military power as a means of political domination. On October 14, when Powell spoke at a 100th birthday celebration for Eisenhower (who died in 1969) in Abilene, Kansas, he articulated his support for restraint: "General Eisenhower," said Powell, "was no proponent of war. He was a proponent of peace. At the foot of the great statue here at the library we see the words 'Champion of Peace.' And so he was."[22]

A week later Powell was in Riyadh, Saudi Arabia, to confer with General Schwarzkopf, the commander-in-chief of U.S. forces in Saudi Arabia. Powell and Schwarzkopf estimated the numbers and kinds of reinforcements they would need to defend Saudi Arabia and also what would be necessary, in the event of war, to defeat the Iraqis.

10

★
THE PATH TO WAR AND PEACE
★

WHEN THE UNITED NATIONS VOTED IN NOVEMBER to bar all trade to or from Iraq, experts estimated that sanctions would take six months to destroy the Iraqi economy and Saddam Hussein. Powell, although he supported sanctions, wasn't sure they would work. Eventually, he believed, a fight would be necessary.

The U.N. passed a resolution on the last day of November authorizing the use of force to eject Iraq from Kuwait if Iraq did not withdraw by January 15. Saddam responded by calling up additional reserves to beef up Iraq's 500,000 deployed troops in Kuwait.

Saddam boasted that Americans would suffer a defeat if they invaded Kuwait to drive his forces out. "Yours is a society," he asserted, "which cannot accept 10,000 dead in one battle." As though to reinforce the point, his spokesmen raised in very unsubtle terms the common and erroneous notion that the United States had suffered a *military*, rather than a political, defeat in Vietnam.[1]

If Saddam Hussein had been better informed

about Powell, however, he would have realized that Powell had less fear of using force than any other American officer since Vietnam. Powell was a political and military strategist. His doctrine was to avoid war if possible, but when engagement was ordered, to throw enough firepower into the fight to win quickly and decisively before antiwar sentiment in the American public could paralyze the military effort. He also believed that the United States had to send a signal that it was still a superpower.

In early December, with millions watching on television, Powell warned Saddam at a news conference, "Don't try to scare us or threaten us. It won't work, never has."[2]

At a Senate Armed Services Committee hearing on December 3, Powell contradicted editorials and inferences by Senator Sam Nunn of Georgia that he was either rushing the president into a narrow military decision or that he was reluctant to tell the president the truth. He also criticized former defense officials, such as his predecessor at the Joint Chiefs, retired Admiral William Crowe, who suggested in television interviews that he was concealing from the president and other military chiefs deep-seated reservations about the possibility of conflict.

Powell noted that he had met with all the service chiefs "some thirty times" in the last four months and that he had met with them individually each day. "I am not reluctant or afraid to give either the Secretary of Defense, the President or any other members of the National Security Council my best, most honest, most candid advice, whether they like it or not. And on—on some occasions, they do not like it."[3]

"Isn't that right?" asked Powell of Cheney, who sat beside him.

"I will confirm that," Cheney said.

The committee broke into laughter.

"Which part, sir?" Powell asked.

"All of it, Colin," Cheney replied.[4]

Congress adopted a nonbinding policy statement December 4 by a vote of 177–37 that President Bush should not initiate any offensive military action in the Persian Gulf without the formal approval of Congress unless American lives were in immediate danger.

Powell, in Britain while the vote took place, met with the new British Prime Minister, John Major, and assured the United States' ally that Americans had not lost their nerve. He also rebutted the impression given in some British newspapers that the United States was looking for a fight. "The only acceptable outcome," Powell told a lunchtime group of British generals, scholars, and policymakers, "is total withdrawal of Iraqi forces from all of Kuwait."[5]

On December 18, President Bush insisted that he was flexible with respect to a negotiated settlement, but he warned that Iraq must quit "every square inch" of Kuwait by January 15 or face war.[6]

Powell had a clear-eyed, relaxed view of the crisis. "I'm not a bookmaker," he said. "I don't know whether there will be a war in the Middle East. . . . I hope one day he [Saddam Hussein] will take a hard look at what his handicap is and say, 'This isn't worth the game. I'm outta here.' "[7]

Powell was in Saudi Arabia just before Christmas, where he addressed a cheering throng of A-10 "Warthog" pilots at an air base: "When we launch it, we will launch it violently, we will launch it massively, so there will be no doubt when it's over who won." And though Powell was painfully aware of the suffering of war, he felt the need to raise the fighting spirits of his troops and encourage them not to fear the worst. "It's gonna be fun," he declared in words that dared Saddam Hussein to fight, "if you ever get started."[8]

To the "jugheads" or "grunts"—the rank-and-file troops—Powell was a leader with whom they could identify. When he visited Saudi Arabia in December, he sat down with 101st Airborne assault troops, a unit in the vanguard of action in the last three wars.

"I know what it's like to be away from your families for the holidays," he said to the troops, over a cold ready-to-eat squish (food paste in a plastic squeeze tube) of chicken à la king. "But this is important work. Stay with us; we'll take care of your families and we'll get you home as fast as we can."[9]

As the United States sought to mediate the dispute through the French, the Russians, and U.N. Secretary General Javier Pérez de Cuéllar, Saddam made a series of grievous mistakes. His first was to misread the American people as a pacifist nation unwilling to fight. His second was to deploy his army in fixed defensive positions and fail completely to anticipate a surprise flanking attack organized by Powell and Schwarzkopf.

Just after New Year's Day, President Bush offered Saddam one last chance to withdraw from Kuwait, but the Iraqi leader refused to budge. Three days later Congress voted the president the power to wage war.

"Strike suddenly," Powell advised the president. "Do it quickly, and do it with minimum loss of life."[10]

At 11 A.M. Tuesday, January 15, Powell received the president's written authorization to use force. At 4:50 P.M. Wednesday, January 16, the first fighter planes took off from Dhahran air base in Saudi Arabia.

Twenty-four hours after the war began, Powell was still in his huge, dimly lit office. In the dark early hours of morning he slipped out of his green dress uniform and pulled a blanket over himself before falling asleep. As he slept on the leather couch that night, his men carried out one of the most systematic destructions of an army ever witnessed anywhere at any time in history. Powell learned that allied planes flew 3,000 sorties (attacks)—a record number for the period—with thirty-three of the first thirty-six radar-evading Stealth missiles hitting bull's-eyes. Allied losses of planes numbered fewer than a handful.

Two days after the war started, President Bush

played his role as commander-in-chief in a top-security room at the Pentagon. Surrounded by Powell and his other advisers, he looked tense and nervous. Every few minutes he looked up from a video monitor of events in the Gulf to ask a question. Seldom had the president seemed to Powell and the others so nervous as he was that day in the War Room.

The president scarcely permitted his advisers to reply to a previous question before he asked another one. Bush wanted to know how much damage the Iraqis had suffered. What were U.S. plans for handling prisoners of war. How was the Air-Land strategy, as the Pentagon labeled it, working?

Throughout the barrage of questions, Powell continued his business with quiet confidence. Each time the president asked a question, Powell replied in a calm, precise manner. But the tension in the room was difficult to conceal. After a half-hour had passed, Bush abruptly broke off the questioning, stood, and in a mock-serious tone announced: "Hey, I'm going to have to do more micromanaging of this thing." The room exploded in laughter, and Powell laughed loudest of all.[11]

Powell slept in his office for six nights straight after the deployment of allied troops. Most of the time, he slept soundly. Often, however, he tossed and turned in sudden fear for the young lives he ordered into danger. During the first week of the war he would have slept no more soundly at home. His concern for his troops grew out of his character rather than followed from his sense of duty. At least in his office he was able to monitor the invasion from Schwarzkopf's stream of bulletins.

Of course, Powell had critics. Some charged that he should have allowed his Marine force to deploy heavily armored units at the same time the lightly armed 82nd Airborne landed in Saudi Arabia. William J. Taylor, one of Powell's former war college instructors, complained that Powell lacked a well-thought-out plan to win and also lacked a sense of urgency.

In strong language, Powell told one of Taylor's grad students that Taylor was wrong.[12] Powell's unified command AirLand strategy was a precise air assault to destroy the enemy's communications and supplies, followed by massive armored attacks on land. The strategy was prevailing against the Iraqis. Powell saw no need to waste innocent American lives with risky tank assaults when missiles and air power could achieve the same end without high casualties.

Before domestic critics had a chance to rally antiwar sentiment, the United States had launched a massive, no-holds-barred attack, depriving Iraq, the weaker military power, of domestic and international political allies.

Since Saddam's army lay well protected in the Kuwaiti desert, Powell aimed to deprive the Iraqis of the ability to communicate with one another. Almost as if Powell were boxing against a blinded slugger, he jabbed at his opponent's eyes—Iraq's command posts in Kuwait and Iraq. Slowly, the allies isolated the "brains" of the Iraqi army, destroying deposits of food and ammunition, and drained the confidence of Iraqi troops who had been told by Saddam, "Should the Americans become embroiled, we will make them swim in their own blood, God willing."[13]

"We have a toolbox that's full of lots of tools," Powell said on February 2. "And I brought them all to the party."[14]

As the events of a hundred succeeding days would show, that response was no idle boast. An icy-cool strategist, Powell had spent five months planning for war, and he now enjoyed the satisfaction of seeing his plans in action. Clearly, the president had left the complex military operation altogether in Powell's hands. Whether defeating Iraq took one month or six mattered little to Powell. He was confident of the outcome. Desert Storm could be quick and painless, or it could be bloody and protracted. But come what might, the president plainly intended to stick by the decisions of his chairman of the Joint Chiefs of Staff.

At a press conference February 6, the nation once again—in the space of just over a year—saw Powell explaining the purpose and extent of a U.S. military operation. Asked by one reporter what the first objective of the U.S. military would be, Powell replied crisply: "First we will cut off the Iraqi army, then we will kill it."[15]

When Powell appeared before the nation, he not only provided a report of the war but also gave assurance to critics and fearful Americans alike that the conflict's outcome did not depend on Saddam. It did not matter that Saddam Hussein refused to surrender. Powell's direct address was intended to reassure the public's faith in its fighting force.

"Trust me," he said, and in large measure a grateful nation did just that.[16]

"His dignity," wrote Roger Starr in *The New York Times*, "candor and restraint commanded respect" the night be told the nation how well the troops in the Persian Gulf were performing. "Was there anyone," asked Starr, "left in my country who, whatever one's views of war, would have felt more comfortable saluting an empty uniform than the black man who wore it last night?"[17] By "empty uniform," Starr was referring to the days of segregated armed forces, when white soldiers were advised to make believe they were saluting an empty uniform rather than a black superior officer.

Powell's popularity soared. Public perception of the man showed him to be modest for someone with such awesome power. When he learned that *U.S. News & World Report* was going to run his photo on the cover of the February 4 issue, he tried to persuade the editors to put General Schwarzkopf on its cover instead.

During the first weeks of the war, Powell questioned his aides for information as much as he commanded them. An aide to Army Chief of Staff General Carl E. Vuono reported that a visitor could expect to be interrupted every twenty minutes by Powell's calls to Vuono's office. Pete Williams, the Pentagon's chief spokesman, was in touch hourly with Powell, an unusual amount of contact that could be demanding and fractious.

"He doesn't often express annoyance or anger," said Powell's aide Colonel Frederick W. Smullen II. But when Powell is upset, watch out. "Sometimes it's just a look,"[18] but an unmistakable, withering look, said Smullen, who should know. But when the dispute involved subordinates, Powell took no quarter, said Smullen, testifying to Powell's decisiveness in dealing with insubordination.

As the air campaign intensified, someone in the Pentagon leaked to a television news report that the United States had a secret new technique for targeting Iraqi tanks. The report sent Powell into a fuming rage. And Smullen took the brunt of Powell's anger, a sharp and profane chewing out for the leak even though Powell knew Smullen was not to blame.

"His anger is intense but short-lived," said Smullen. "It lasts seconds, not minutes."[19]

Iraq, trapped by mounting losses, tried a last-ditch ploy. On February 23, Saddam Hussein offered to withdraw from Kuwait in return for an Israeli withdrawal from the West Bank in Gaza, the removal of all allied troops from the Gulf area, and payment or reparations for allied bomb damage to Iraq. The Bush administration immediately denounced the offer as a "cruel hoax."[20]

On February 28, the allied ground attack plan was activated officially. President Bush wanted to escape the pressures at the White House, so he and

Powell went to Ford's Theater to see *Black Eagles*, a play about black World War II airmen.

At 10:20 P.M. Bush met with Powell and other advisers in the president's private study on the second floor of the White House residence. Powell and the others studied a pair of freshly copied documents from Mikhail Gorbachev, who had offered to mediate the dispute, and a letter from the Iraqi foreign minister, reiterating Saddam Hussein's defiance. All in the room agreed that the terms set forth by Saddam Hussein were unacceptable. In Powell's hands were papers awaiting the president's signature for the commencement of a land invasion, called operation Desert Sabre. Bush looked at Powell's plans and authorization.

Bush scanned the papers, nodded, and said: "I like both of these."[21]

"Well, let's set a date and set a time," suggested Powell.

"I think that's a good idea," Bush replied immediately. Powell added that a deadline would be "helpful to the military because then my guys in the field know what to expect. They know exactly what to be looking for and when."

The president, Powell, and others agreed on Saturday noon, March 2, as the time and date for the ground offensive.

"What's it do for you, Colin?" asked the president.

"It's good for me," said Powell.[22]

In the first twenty-two hours, 23,000 Iraqi troops surrendered. "This is the boringest war I've ever seen," said Sergeant Addison Wembley. "They just keep dropping their gear and raising their hands. I've seen hundreds of them."[23]

Less than a week after the ground war had begun, Bush went on the air to announce that he was ordering a suspension of all offensive actions. It was six weeks after the U.N. deadline of January 15. Finally, Iraq agreed to accept U.N. terms for unconditional surrender and withdrawal from Kuwait.

After the Persian Gulf victory, Powell addressed the Veterans of Foreign Wars in Washington. He reminded them that he had told them right after Iraq invaded Kuwait that Saddam's threats would never deter American will.

"Was I right?" Powell asked, standing before a wall-size American flag.[24] The crowd roared with approval.

In the aftermath of Powell's triumph, he emerged from the war with the image of a national hero. He seemed to embody patriotism, racial justice, and technical brilliance—qualities any civilized nation would prize.

11

★
A MAN FOR ALL SEASONS
★

PERHAPS IN NO OTHER AREA OF AMERICAN LIFE HAS the rise of Colin Powell symbolized so much promise as in matters pertaining to race.

Light-skinned Powell has proudly identified himself with black Americans rather than a subgroup of black Americans, as have many West Indian islanders and African immigrants. He is a member of the Army Rocks, an organization of black officers, and he is a student of African-American history, especially the history of blacks in the armed services.

"I am an American black," he says, "and . . . I am flattered that people would say that in me there is an example of what can be achieved in this country."[1]

When he was winding up his stint as national security adviser, Powell attended a White House state dinner. He was sitting down at a table when a black waiter, a veteran, walked over to him.

"General," the waiter said. "I know you're leaving. I just wanted to thank you and say it's been good to see you here. I was in World War II, and I fought all the way from North Africa to Italy."

"Brother," the general replied, "I ought to be thanking you."[2]

Asked at a congressional hearing about the disproportionate number of blacks serving in the military, Powell said the armed forces were a way of moving up in society. "I ain't done too bad," he quipped dryly.[3]

The Boston Globe's Washington bureau correspondent, Michael K. Frisby, wrote in 1991: "With an adroit use of social, political and military skills, General Colin Luther Powell [is] the most powerful African American in the nation's history. Yet this South Bronx native has largely avoided the biting criticism that many successful blacks in government and private industry attract—the accusation that he has sold out his own people to gain an influential position with whites."[4]

Indeed, Powell has not forgotten his roots. After the Gulf War, Powell returned to his alma mater, Morris High School, in the South Bronx. His appearance there made front-page news. "I remember the front door," he said to the assembled students in the school's gymnasium. "I remember the auditorium. I remember the feeling that you can't make it. But you can." Then he said: "Forget everything else. Let's just talk. Things have changed, but you didn't discover everything."[5]

He encouraged the students to avoid drugs and get their diplomas. "Stick with it," he said. "I'm giving you an order. Stick with it. Stay in high school and get that diploma. Don't do drugs, it's stupid. . . . Don't think you are limited by your background. Challenges are there to be knocked down."[6]

It was the first time he had returned to the school in thirty-seven years. He took a tour of Kelly Street, where he recalled that even when he was in high school, local drug dealers worked the street. He was presented with a cap, sweatsuit, and trophy by Elliott Lopez, a junior and member of the same track team that Powell had been a member of in 1950–54. Another student presented Powell with a collection of Desert Storm trading cards and said to him: "You've worked hard. Relax and chill out."[7]

When he talks to black school children, his message is: Work hard! "In the Army," he once said, "I never felt I was looked down on by my white colleagues. I've been given the opportunity to compete fair and square with them, and if some don't like this, that is not Colin Powell's problem. It's their problem."[8]

"We don't tolerate drugs. We'll go to any extent to stamp them out," he said. "That's the kind of approach you have to have to drugs.

"In our schools, we must have discipline and we must have high standards. In our schools, we need to motivate our children. I know a school can't be run like an infantry platoon but it seemed pretty much like that where I went to school."[9]

He noted how easily American troops of all racial, religious, and ethnic backgrounds mingled and were molded into a "family" in the Gulf. He voiced the hope that the same "family" sense could become a reality in the United States. "We would come to know that we depend on one another, we would come to know that we all are family," he said to loud cheers of approbation.[10]

Since the allied victory in the Persian Gulf, political commentators have published speculations on Powell's future as a vice-presidential or presidential candidate. More than one commentator has written of a Bush-Powell ticket in 1992 as the Republicans' "Dream Ticket." Tom Wicker wrote,

> The Dream Ticket, that perennial fantasy of American politics, is again showing a pretty face and an alluring smile. This time the dream has President Bush paired with General Colin Powell, the black Chairman of the Joint Chiefs of Staff, as his running mate in 1992.
>
> Now that General Powell has directed the military to its runaway victory in the Persian Gulf war, this Dream Ticket is even more attractive than when first proposed in 1988. The general was then only Ronald Reagan's national security adviser.[11]

The *Boston Globe*'s Derrick Z. Jackson wrote, "No recent presidential candidate has been so easy to predict so far in advance as General Colin L. Powell. . . . He is a walking United States flag. He has stars on his shoulders and stripes on his chest.

His snappy confidence is unripped by media gales."[12]

What impressed Jackson most was Powell's authority at the Pentagon press conferences alongside Dick Cheney. When "asked how the U.S. could claim air superiority over Iraq," wrote Jackson, Powell responded: " 'I used to teach the subject. I own the JCS [Joint Chiefs of Staff] publication that has the definition in it, which I helped write when I was a captain. And I can assure you that this qualifies for the definition of air superiority.' "[13]

"The media offered no further challenge that day," wrote Jackson. "Powell is perfect for a 'Superior America' in 1996."

Jackson noted that Powell appeals to whites and blacks, military conservatives and political liberals, Democrats and conservative Republicans, Jesse Jackson and North Carolina's conservative Republican Senator, Jesse Helms, who said, "I can't think of anyone who is critical of him."

According to Jackson, "No other African-American, other than an athlete or an entertainer, commands that breadth of respect. For the better part of two centuries, the U.S. military sent African-Americans off to war and returned them to lynchings, segregation and limited employment. By the beginning of the twenty-first century, the armed forces just might give us our first African-American president."[14]

Powell has been called a "black Eisenhower," after the World War II general who was the supreme allied commander and who later became a two-term

Republican president. Yet despite the comparison and the fact that Powell has served in three Republican administrations, Powell keeps his politics to himself and is a registered Independent. However, he has advised Democratic presidential candidate Jesse Jackson and Chairman of the Democratic National Committee Ron Brown.

Journalist and historian Roger Wilkins of George Mason University recalled that at a party, as he was about to introduce his wife, Patricia, to Powell, the general abruptly said to Wilkins, "You don't have to introduce me to her. I know her. I worked with her when she worked for HEW, and I was detailed to the budget office in the early 1970s."[15]

"Powell is a politician in the old-fashioned, buy-you-a-hot-dog style, that's true," said one official in 1991.[16] Not only has Powell a politician's memory for names, but he has a sense of timing and ability to tell an audience what he thinks will win it over. In an address to a Jewish lobbying group, Powell joked, "I don't speak Yiddish." Then he smiled and added, "Well, maybe a bissel," using the Yiddish expression for "just a little." According to Frisby, "the crowd loved it."[17]

And it's not only his own country that has gone crazy for Powell. The British also have a thing for him. Former Prime Minister Margaret Thatcher's foreign policy adviser, Sir Charles Powell, admires the general, calling him "cousin."[18] He also once called Powell the most impressive American soldier he had ever met.

Powell has been lionized in the British press, with daily articles emphasizing his British roots (Jamaica was a British colony). One *London Times* columnist, Colin Dunne, who proudly claims a spiritual connection with Powell based on their common forename, trumpets his connection to the general.

"In a book of babies' names," wrote Dunne, "I found news to cheer Colins the world over—and the general more than most. The name [Colin] means 'victorious.' Colin the Victorious. With a name like that, Powell can pronounce it any old way he wants. Talk about the right man for the job. . . ."[19]

Powell is a military-history buff, who previewed the PBS series *The Civil War* and gave a video of the documentary as a gift to President Bush. He is still a fan of actors Gary Cooper, Cary Grant, and Gregory Peck, and he still enjoys watching westerns and thrillers. Although his favorite pastime is repairing old Volvos, he has a hard time indulging himself.

The Gulf War forced Powell to cancel his appearance as grand marshal for Atlanta's Martin Luther King, Jr., Memorial parade on January 21, 1991, but after the war he threw the first ball at a Yankees–White Sox game, appeared on a prime-time television tribute to Gulf troops, and led a grand parade in Chicago.

All of the Powells have adjusted well to their new celebrity status. Besides Powell's being mentioned as a possible vice-presidential candidate, his wife, Alma, and his daughter Linda, an actress who appeared as a law student in the 1990 film *Reversal of Fortune,* have become items in the gossip columns.

In May 1991, President Bush reappointed Powell for a second two-year term as chairman of the Joint Chiefs. The story of Colin Luther Powell continues to develop, and perhaps his greatest personal achievements are still to come. But what is known about him up to now only enhances his reputation. He has survived the fortunes of war, and in the bargain he has brought honor to all those associated with him in keeping the peace. Most of his country, not surprisingly, admires him.

★
CHRONOLOGICAL SUMMARY
★

Life and Career Highlights of
General Colin Luther Powell

Date and place of birth: April 5, 1937, New York, New York.

Parents: Luther Theophilus and Maud Ariel McKoy Powell of Jamaica.

Early education (1942–53): P.S. No. 39; Morris High School, South Bronx, New York City.

Educational degrees: City University of New York, Bachelor of Science (Geology), and Reserve Officers Training Corps, June 9, 1958; George Washington University, Master of Business Administration, Washington, D.C., July, 1971.

August 24, 1962: Marriage to Alma Vivian Johnson of Birmingham, Alabama. Three children.

Years of active commissioned service: Over thirty-five.

Major assignments:
- June 1958–October 1958: 2nd Lieutenant, Infantry, Ranger and Airborne, Fort Benning, Georgia.

CHRONOLOGICAL SUMMARY ★ 122

- May 1959–July 1959: 1st Lieutenant, Combat Command B, 3rd Armored Division, Europe.
- February 1962–September 1962: Captain, 1st Battalion, 2nd Infantry, 5th Infantry (Mechanized), Fort Devens, Massachusetts.
- December 1962–November 1963: Senior Battalion Advisor, I Corps, 1st Infantry Division, Army of The Republic of Vietnam, Military Assistance Advisory Group, Vietnam. Wounded in action and decorated. Awarded Purple Heart.
- March 23, 1963: Son, Michael, is born.
- April 16, 1965: Daughter Linda is born.
- February 1966–June 1967: Major, instructor/author, United States Army Infantry School, Fort Benning, Georgia.
- June 1968–July 1969: Executive Officer, 3rd Battalion, 1st Infantry, 11th Infantry Brigade, Americal Division; Assistant Chief of Staff, Deputy of Operations, Americal Division, United States Army, Vietnam.
- July 1970–June 1979: promoted to Lieutenant Colonel, Colonel (Temporary in February 1976), Brigadier General (Temporary until January 22, 1982).
- May 20, 1971: Daughter Annmarie is born.
- 1972: Chosen to be a White House Fellow.
- September 1972–August 1973: White House Fellow, Office of Management and Budget, The White House, Washington, D.C.
- September 1973–September 1974: Commander, 1st Battalion, 32nd Infantry, 2nd Infantry Division, Eighth United States Army, Korea.

CHRONOLOGICAL SUMMARY ★ 123

- September 1974–July 1975: Operations Research Systems Analyst, Defense Department, Washington, D.C.
- April 1976–July 1977: Commander, 2nd Brigade, 101st Airborne Division (Air Assault), Fort Campbell, Kentucky.
- July 1977–June 1981: Special Assignments (Classified), Defense Department, Washington, D.C.
- June 1981–August 1982: Assistant Division Commander, 4th Infantry Division (Mechanized), Fort Carson, Colorado.
- August 1982–June 1986: Deputy Commanding General, United States Army Combined Arms Combat Development Activity, Fort Leavenworth, Kansas. Promoted to Lieutenant General July 1, 1986.
- July 1983–June 1986: Military Assistant to the Secretary of Defense, Washington, D.C.
- June 1986–December 1986: Commanding General, V Corps, United States Army, Europe.
- January 1987–December 1987: Deputy Assistant to the President for National Security Affairs, The White House, Washington, D.C.
- December 1987–January 1989: Full Three-star General, Assistant to the President for National Security Affairs, The White House, Washington, D.C.
- April 1989–September 1989: Commander-in-Chief, Forces Command, Fort McPherson, Georgia.
- December 20, 1989: Directs U.S. invasion of

Panama in successful overthrow and capture of General Manuel Noriega.
- October 1989 to present: Chairman of the Joint Chiefs of Staff, Washington, D.C.
- January 15, 1991: Heads United States and United Nations in military defeat and expulsion of Saddam Hussein's Iraqi Army from Kuwait in 100 days.
- April 4, 1991: Appointed Four-star General.

Principal decorations: Awarded two Purple Heart Medals, Bronze Star Medal, Air Medal, Soldier's Medal, Legion of Merit with Oak Leaf Cluster, Joint Service Commendation Medal, Presidential Service Medal, Defense Distinguished Service Medal with two Oak Leaf Clusters, Army Commendation medal with two Oak Leaf Clusters, Congressional Gold Medal, President's Citizens Medal, Presidential Medal of Freedom, Secretary of Energy Distinguished Service Medal, Distinguished Service Medal, U.S. Army.

★ Source Notes ★

Chapter 1

1. Marilyn Powell Berns, telephone interviews with author, May–June 1991.
2. Ibid.
3. Colin Powell, interview by Marilyn MacKay, Sept. 17, 1990 (Wash., D.C.: Alderson Reporting Co.), 11.
4. Ibid.
5. Richard Mackenzie, "Pulled to the Top by His Bootstraps," *Insight* (Oct. 8, 1990): 10.
6. Simeon Booker, "Black General at the Summit of U.S. Power," *Ebony* (July 1988): 146.
7. Mackenzie, 10. Also see Rick Hampson, "The General's Bloc: Tracing Gen. Powell's Roots," New York: The Associated Press, Feb. 9, 1991, and "Powell Sets British Straight," *The New York Times*, Apr. 27, 1991.
8. Colin L. Powell, "From CCNY to the White House," *The Public Interest* 94 (Winter 1989): 88.
9. Rose Blue and Corinne J. Nadeau, *Colin*

Powell: Straight to the Top (Brookfield, CT: The Millbrook Press, 1991), 12.

10. Mackenzie, 10.
11. Blue and Nadeau, 12.
12. Mackenzie, 11.
13. Saul Friedman, "Four-Star Warrior," *Long Island Newsday Magazine*, Feb. 11, 1990, sec. A.
14. Carl T. Rowan, "Called to Service: The Colin Powell Story," *Reader's Digest* (Dec. 1989): 122 and Powell, "White House," 87–88.

Chapter 2

1. Powell, "White House," 87.
2. Ibid.
3. Blue and Nadeau, 18.
4. Rowan, 122.
5. Roi Ottley and William J. Weatherby, eds., *The Negro in New York: An Informal Social History* (New York: The New York Public Library, 1967), xvii.
6. Powell, interview by MacKay, 15.
7. Mackenzie, 11.

Chapter 3

1. Paula Lee Potts, "A Conversation With Alma Powell," *Military Lifestyle* (May 1990): 38ff.
2. Potts, 39.
3. Andrew Rosenthal, "A General Who Is

Right for His Time," *The New York Times*, Aug. 10, 1991, sec. A.
    4. Simeon Booker, "Black General," 144.
    5. Ibid.
    6. James L. Binder, "Gen. Colin L. Powell," *Army*, Apr. 1990: 22.
    7. Potts, 38.
    8. Rowan, 122.

Chapter 4

    1. Rowan, 122.
    2. According to a Defense Department chart, categories of ground combat units for the Army have the following size and place in a hierarchy of troop organization and rank of commander at each level:

1. *Type:* squad. *Total soldiers:* 9–12. *Commanded by:* staff sergeant.
2. *Type:* platoon. *Components:* three squads. *Total soldiers:* approx. 30. *Commanded by:* lieutenant. (*Insignia by rank:* 2nd lieutenant, single gold bar; 1st lieutenant, single silver bar.)
3. *Type:* company. *Components:* three to four platoons. *Total soldiers:* 100–130. *Commanded by:* captain. (*Insignia by rank:* Captain: two silver bars; major: gold oak leaf.)
4. *Type:* battalion. *Components:* three to five companies. *Total soldiers:* 500–750. *Commanded by:* lieutenant colonel. (*Insignia by rank:* silver oak leaf.)

5. *Type:* brigade/regiment. *Components:* two to five battalions plus support units. *Total soldiers:* 1,800–4,000. *Commanded by:* colonel. (*Insignia by rank:* silver eagle.)

6. *Type:* division. *Components:* three brigades plus support units. *Total soldiers:* 11,000–17,000. *Commanded by:* major general. (*Insignia by rank:* brigadier general, one silver star; major general, two silver stars.)

7. *Type:* corps. *Components:* two or more divisions plus support units. *Total soldiers:* 50,000–100,000. *Commanded by:* lieutenant general. (*Insignia by rank:* lieutenant general, three silver stars; general, four silver stars; general of the Army, five silver stars.)

3. Powell, interview by MacKay, 25.

4. Benjamin Quarles, *The Negro in the Making of America* (New York: Collier Macmillan Publishers, 1987), 287.

5. David Wallechinsky, " 'Have a Vision,' " *Parade* (Aug. 14, 1989): A4.

6. Rowan, 123.

7. Ibid.

8. Ibid.

9. Rudy Abramson and John Broder, "Four-Star Power," *Los Angeles Times Magazine*, Apr. 7, 1991: 60.

10. Friedman, sec. A.

11. "Gen. Colin Powell's Advice To Young Blacks Today: Prepare and Be Ready," *Jet* (Sept. 11, 1989): 14.

12. Mackenzie, 12.
13. Ibid., 13.

Chapter 5

1. Powell, interview by Mackay, 10.
2. Friedman, sec. A.
3. Booker, "Black General," 146.
4. Ibid.
5. Ibid.
6. Lou Cannon, "Gen. Powell Regarded as Steady, Realistic," *The Washington Post*, Aug. 10, 1989, sec. A.
7. Mackenzie, 14.
8. Rowan, 124.
9. Ibid.
10. Ibid.
11. Ibid.
12. Ibid.
13. Ibid.
14. Richard Mackenzie, p. 14.
15. Ibid.
16. Rowan, 124.
17. Powell, interview by MacKay, 22.
18. Ibid.
19. Ibid.
20. Ibid.
21. Friedman, sec. A.

Chapter 6

1. Booker, "Black General," 136.
2. Ibid., 140.

3. Ibid.
4. Friedman, sec. A.
5. James M. Blount, "Lt. General Colin L. Powell: Monitoring the World's Hot Spots," *about . . . time* (May, 1988): 10.
6. Ibid.
7. Rowan, 125.
8. Ibid.
9. Powell, interview by MacKay, 13.
10. Blount, 10–12.
11. Blount, 12.
12. Carl T. Rowan, 125.
13. Blount, 10.
14. Wallechinsky, p. 19.
15. Ibid.
16. Blount, 12.
17. Ibid.
18. Ibid.
19. Ibid., 13.
20. Ibid.
21. MacKenzie, 12.

Chapter 7

1. "The NBC Nightly News," Dec. 31, 1988.
2. Rowan, 125.
3. Rowan, 125.
4. Blount, 13.
5. Mackenzie, 15.
6. Rowan, 125.
7. Ann Devroy and George C. Wilson, "Bush

Picks 'Complete Soldier' Powell to Head the Joint Chiefs," *The Washington Post*, Aug. 11, 1989, sec. A.

8. Ibid.

9. Melissa Healy, "Powell Honors Blacks Who Served," *The Los Angeles Times*, Aug. 18, 1989, 4. Also see Reuters, "Powell Links His Rise to All Black Soldiers," *The New York Times*, Aug. 18, 1989, sec. A.

10. Gwen Ifill, "Armed Forces Making Strides, Powell Says," *The Washington Post*, Aug. 18, 1989, sec. A.

11. Ibid.

12. Healy, 4; Ifill, sec. A.

13. "Gen. Powell's Advice," 12. Contrast *Jet*'s report with Melissa Healy's of *The Los Angeles Times* and Gwen Ifill's of *The Washington Post* (see above, notes 9 and 10). Healy quoted Powell as saying, "But now that we're on top and looking over that cliff, there are still more rivers to cross." Ifill quotes him saying, "There are still more rivers to be crossed."

14. "Gen. Powell's Advice," 12.

15. Ifill, sec. A.

16. Ibid.

17. Ibid.

18. Devroy and Wilson, sec. A.

19. Bruce W. Nelan, "Ready for Action," *Time* (Nov. 12, 1990): 28.

20. "Gen. Powell's Advice," 13; and Cannon, sec. A.

21. "Gen. Powell's Advice," 13.

22. Ibid., 14.
23. Mackenzie, 12.
24. Bob Woodward, *The Commanders* (New York: Simon and Schuster, 1991), 153.

Chapter 8

1. Bob Woodward, "The Conversion of General Powell," *The Washington Post*, Dec. 21, 1989, sec. A.
2. Friedman, sec. A.
3. Woodward, *Commanders*, 125–26.
4. Woodward, "Conversion," sec. A.
5. Woodward, *Commanders*, 178.
6. Susan Watters, "The General's Lady," *Ebony* (Sept. 1991): 52.
7. Woodward, *Commanders*, 187.
8. Associated Press, "Excerpts from the Pentagon Briefing," *The New York Times*, Dec. 21, 1991, sec. A.
9. Associated Press, sec. A; Woodward, *Commanders*, 189.
10. Friedman, sec. A.
11. Ibid.
12. Andy Pasztor, "Powell Was Perfectly Cast to Plan and Explain Assault," *The Wall Street Journal*, Dec. 21, 1989, sec. A.

Chapter 9

1. Friedman, sec. A.
2. Caspar W. Weinberger, "General Colin Powell—an Inside View," *Forbes* (Jan. 22, 1990): 31.

3. George C. Wilson, "Sweeping Restructuring of Military to Be Powell's Mission as New Chief," *The Washington Post*, Sept. 30, 1989, sec. A.

4. James Feron, "An 'Old General' Talks of Pride at West Point," *The New York Times*, June 1, 1990, sec. B.

5. Ibid.

6. Ibid.

7. Ibid.

8. Ibid.

9. Patrick E. Tyler, "Powell Resists Deeper Pentagon Cuts," *The Washington Post*, June 23, 1990, sec. A.

10. Ibid.

11. Bruce W. Nelan, "Call to Arms," *Time* (Sept. 24, 1990): 33.

12. Andy Pasztor and Gerald F. Seib, "Cool Commander: Force in Gulf Reflects Colin Powell's Vision," *The Wall Street Journal*, Oct. 15, 1990, sec. A.

13. Andrew Rosenthal, "Military Chief: Man of Action and of Politics," *The New York Times*, Aug. 17, 1990, sec. A.

14. Mackenzie, 15.

15. Tom Matthews et al., "The Path to War," *Newsweek* (Spring/Summer 1991): 40.

16. Mackenzie, 8.

17. Mackenzie, 9.

18. Michael R. Gordon, "Top Soviet General Tells U.S. Not to Attack in Gulf," *The New York Times*, Oct. 3, 1990, sec. A.

19. Andrew Rosenthal, "Military Chief," sec. A.
20. Ibid.
21. Matthews et al., 45.
22. Woodward, *Commanders*, 307.

Chapter 10

1. George J. Church, "Saddam's Options," *Time* (Jan. 2, 1991): 29.
2. Patrick E. Tyler, "Cheney Authorizes Mobilization of 49,703 Reservists; General Powell Issues Warning to Saddam," *The Washington Post*, Aug. 24, 1990, sec. A.
3. Woodward, *Commanders*, 341–343.
4. Ibid., 343.
5. Craig R. Whitney, "Powell Tells British U.S. Still Has Nerve to Oppose the Iraqis," *The New York Times*, Dec. 5, 1990, sec. A.
6. Jessica Lee, "Bush: Door Still Open On Talks," *USA Today*, Dec. 18, 1990: 1.
7. Jessica Lee, "Will There Be War? 'I'm Not a Bookmaker,' " *USA Today*, Dec. 18, 1990: 1.
8. Abramson and Broder, 20.
9. Tom Post et al., "A Commanding Presence," *Newsweek* (Spring/Summer 1991): 83.
10. David Harbrecht et al., "Managing the War," *Business Week* (Feb. 4, 1991): 35.
11. Ibid., 34.
12. Post et al., 83. ("Tell Taylor," said Powell, "I want to kick him. . . .")

13. Michael Kramer, "The Moment of Truth," *Time* (Jan. 21, 1991): 24.

14. Bruce B. Auster, "In the Footsteps of Two Georges," *U.S. News & World Report* (Feb. 4, 1991): 26.

15. John Keegan, " 'Cut It Off, then Kill It,' " *The Providence Journal Bulletin*, Mar. 3, 1991, Op-Ed.

16. Auster, 26.

17. Roger Starr, "A Salute for a Man and a Uniform," *The New York Times*, Jan. 18, 1991, sec. A.

18. Abramson and Broder, 60.

19. Ibid.

20. George J. Church, "Saddam's Endgame," *Time* (Feb. 25, 1991): 17.

21. George J. Church, "Marching to a Conclusion: The Night that Bush Decided," *Time* (Mar. 4, 1991): 18–25.

22. Ibid.

23. Jerry Adler, "The Final Push," *Newsweek* (Spring/Summer 1991): 99.

24. Patrick E. Tyler, "The Powell-Cheney Relationship: Blunt Give-and-Take Early in Crisis," *The New York Times*, Mar. 15, 1991, sec. A.

Chapter 11

1. Powell, interview by MacKay, 27.
2. Mackenzie, 12.
3. Maureen Dowd, "Stars of Bush War Coun-

cil Audition for Lead of Next Presidential Battles," *The New York Times*, May 6, 1991, sec. A.

4. Michael K. Frisby, "Colin Powell: At the Top but Mindful of His Roots," *The Boston Globe*, Apr. 21, 1991, sec. A.

5. Craig Wolf, "General Powell Sees the Bronx He Loves, in Memory," *The New York Times*, Apr. 16, 1991, sec. B.

6. Ibid.

7. Ibid.

8. Rowan, 126.

9. Kiernan Crowley, "Powell Gung-Ho for Drug Tests," *The New York Post*, Apr. 17, 1991.

10. Ibid.

11. Tom Wicker, "The Dream Ticket," *The New York Times*, Mar. 6, 1991, sec. A.

12. Derrick Z. Jackson, "Powell in '96?" *The Boston Globe*, Feb. 3, 1991, Op-Ed.

13. Ibid.

14. Ibid.

15. Frisby, sec. A.

16. Ibid.

17. Ibid.

18. Craig R. Whitney, "A Veteran of the Great Tory Wars Exits No. 10," *The New York Times*, Mar. 26, 1991, sec. A.

19. Colin Dunne, "Coe-lin the Victorious," *The London Times*, Feb. 18, 1991.

★
SELECTED BIBLIOGRAPHY
★

Abramson, Rudy, and John Broder. "Four-Star Power." *Los Angeles Times Magazine* (Apr. 7, 1991): 19–58.

Adler, Jerry. "The Final Push." *Newsweek*, Special Issue (Spring/Summer 1991): 99.

Associated Press. "Excerpts from the Pentagon Briefing." *The New York Times* (Dec. 21, 1989) Sec. A.

Auster, Bruce B. "In the Footsteps of Two Georges." *U.S. News & World Report* (Feb. 4, 1991): 26–27.

Binder, James L. "Gen. Colin L. Powell." *Army*, Apr. 1990: 22ff.

Binkin, Martin, and Mark J. Eitelberg. *Blacks in the Military.* Washington, DC: Brookings Institution, 1982.

Blount, James M. "Lt. General Colin L. Powell: Monitoring the World's Hot Spots." about . . . time (May 1988): 10ff.

Blue, Rose, and Corinne J. Nadeau. *Colin Powell: Straight to the Top.* Brookfield, Ct: The Millbrook Press, 1991.

Booker, Simeon. "Black General at the Summit of U.S. Power," *Ebony* (July, 1988): 146ff.

Booker, Simeon. "Black Participation in the War." *Jet* (Feb. 25, 1991): 4–9.

Cannon, Lou. "Gen. Powell Regarded as Steady, Realistic." *The Washington Post* (Aug. 10, 1989): Sec. A.

Church, George J. "Marching to a Conclusion: The Night that Bush Decided." *Time* (Mar. 4, 1991): 18–25.

———. "Saddam's Endgame." *Time* (Feb. 25, 1991): 17ff.

———. "Saddam's Options." *Time* (Jan. 2, 1991): 29.

Crowley, Kiernan. "Powell Gung-Ho for Drug Tests." *The New York Post* (Apr. 17, 1991).

Dalfiume, Richard M. *Desegregation of the United States Armed Forces: Fighting on Two Fronts, 1939–1953.* Columbia: University of Missouri Press, 1969.

Davis, Benjamin O., Jr. *Benjamin O. Davis, Jr., American: An Autobiography.* Washington, DC: Smithsonian Institution, 1991.

Devroy, Ann, and George C. Wilson. "Bush Picks 'Complete Soldier' Powell to Head the Joint Chiefs." *The Washington Post* (Aug. 11, 1989): Sec. A.

Dowd, Maureen. "Stars of Bush War Council Audition for Lead of Next Presidential Battles." *The New York Times* (May 6, 1991): Sec. A.

Dunne, Colin. "Coe-lin the Victorious." *The London Times* (Feb. 18, 1991). Sec. A.

Feron, James. "An 'Old General' Talks of Pride at

West Point." *The New York Times* (June 1, 1990): Sec. B.

Fletcher, Marvin E. *America's First Black General*. Lawrence: University Press of Kansas, 1989.

Fowler, Arlen. *The Black Infantry in the West, 1869–1891*. Westport, CT: Greenwood Press, 1971.

Friedman, Saul. "Four-Star Warrior." *Long Island Newsday Magazine*) Feb. 11, 1990): 10ff.

Frisby, Michael K. "Colin Powell: At the Top but Mindful of His Roots." *The Boston Sunday Globe* (Apr. 21, 1991): Sec. A.

"Gen. Colin Powell's Advice to Young Blacks Today: Prepare and Be Ready." *Jet* (Sept. 11, 1989): 12ff.

Gordon, Michael R. "Top Soviet General Tells U.S. Not to Attack in Gulf." *The New York Times* (Oct. 3, 1990): Sec. A.

Hampson, Rick. "The General's Bloc: Tracing Gen. Powell's Roots." New York: The Associated Press, Feb. 9, 1991.

Harbrecht, David, et al. "Managing the War." *Business Week* (Feb. 4, 1991): 34–37.

Healy, Melissa. "Powell Honors Blacks Who Served." *The Los Angeles Times* (Aug. 18, 1989) Sec. A.

Ifill, Gwen. "Armed Forces Making Strides, Powell Says." *The Washington Post* (Aug. 18, 1989): A11ff.

Jackson, Derrick Z. "Powell in '96?" *The Boston Globe* (Feb. 3, 1991): Op-Ed.

Keegan, John. "Cut It Off, then Kill It." *The Providence Journal-Bulletin* (Mar. 3, 1991): Op-Ed.

Kramer, Michael. "The Moment of Truth." *Time* (Jan. 21, 1991): 23ff.

Leckie, William H. *The Buffalo Soldiers: A Narrative of the Negro Cavalry in the West.* Norman: University of Oklahoma Press, 1985.

Lee, Jessica. "Bush: Door Still Open on Talks." *USA Today* (Dec. 18, 1990): 1.

———. "Will There Be War? 'I'm Not a Bookmaker.' " *USA Today* (Dec. 18, 1990): 1.

Mackenzie, Richard. "Pulled to the Top by His Bootstraps." *Insight* (October 8, 1990): 8–17.

Matthews, Tom, et al. "The Path to War." *Newsweek*, Special Issue (Spring/Summer 1991): 34–48ff.

Motley, Mary. *The Invisible Soldiers: The Experience of the Black Soldier, World War II.* Detroit: Wayne State University Press, 1987.

Nalty, Bernard C. *Strength for the Fight.* New York: Free Press, 1986.

Nelan, Bruce W. "Call to Arms." *Time* (Sept. 24, 1990): 32ff.

———. "Ready for Action." *Time* (Nov. 12, 1990): 26ff.

Ottley, Roi, and William J. Weatherby, eds. *The Negro in New York: An Informal Social History.* New York: The New York Public Library, 1967.

Pasztor, Andy. "Powell Was Perfectly Cast to Plan and Explain Assault." *The Wall Street Journal* (Dec. 21, 1989): Sec. A.

Pasztor, Andy, and Gerald F. Seib. "Cool Commander: Force in Gulf Reflects Colin Powell's Vision; It's Big and It's Mobile." *The Wall Street Journal* (Oct. 15, 1990); Sec. A.

Post, Tom, et al. "A Commanding Presence." *Newsweek*, Special Issue (Spring/Summer 1991): 83.

Potts, Paula Lee. "A Conversation With Alma Powell." *Military Lifestyle* (May 1990): 38ff.

"Powell Sets British Straight." *The New York Times* (Apr. 27, 1991): Sec. A.

Powell, Colin L. "From CCNY to the White House," *The Public Interest* 94 (Winter 1989) 87ff.

———. Interview by Marilyn MacKay. Washington, D. C.: Alderson Reporting Co., Sept. 17, 1990.

Prados, John. *Keepers of the Keys: A History of the National Security Council from Truman to Bush.* New York: Morrow, 1991.

Quarles, Benjamin. *The Negro in the Making of America.* 2nd rev. ed. New York: Collier Macmillan Publishers, 1987.

Reuters. "Powell Links His Rise to All Black Soldiers." *The New York Times* (Aug. 18, 1989): Sec. A.

Rosenthal, Andrew. "A General Who Is Right for His Time." *The New York Times* (Aug. 10, 1991): Sec. A.

———. "Military Chief: Man of Action and of Politics." *The New York Times* (Aug. 17, 1990): Sec. A.

———. "President Bush Praises Black Heroes in Military." *The New York Times* (Feb. 26, 1991): Sec. A.

———. "Will New Helmsman at Joint Chiefs

Weather Tricky Policy Crossroads?" *The New York Times* (Aug. 15, 1989): Sec. A.

Rowan, Carl T. "Called to Service: The Colin Powell Story." *Reader's Digest* (Dec. 1989): 121ff.

Smith, Graham. *When Jim Crow Met John Bull: Black American Soldiers in World War II in Britain.* New York: St. Martin's Press, 1988.

Starr, Roger. "A Salute for a Man and a Uniform." *The New York Times* (Jan. 18, 1991): Sec. A.

Tyler, Patrick E. "Cheney Authorizes Mobilization of 49,703 Reservists; General Powell Issues Warning to Saddam." *The Washington Post* (Aug. 24, 1990): Sec. A.

———. "The Powell-Cheney Relationship: Blunt Give-and-Take Early in Crisis." *The New York Times* (Mar. 15, 1991): Sec. A.

———. "Powell Resists Deeper Pentagon Cuts." *The Washington Post* (June 23, 1990): Sec. A.

Wallechinsky, David. " 'Have a Vision.' " *Parade* (Aug. 14, 1989): A4ff.

Watters, Susan. "The General's Lady." *Ebony* (Sept. 1991): 52.

Weinberger, Caspar W. "General Powell—an Inside View." *Forbes* (Jan. 22, 1990): 31.

Whitney, Craig R. "Powell Tells British U.S. Still Has Nerve to Oppose the Iraqis." *The New York Times* (Dec. 5, 1990): Sec. A.

———. "A Veteran of the Great Tory Wars Exits No. 10. "*The New York Times* (Mar. 26, 1991): Sec. A.

Wilson, George C. "Gen. Powell Due to Lead Joint Chiefs." *The Washington Post* (Aug. 10, 1989): 1ff.

———. "Sweeping Restructuring of Military to Be Powell's Mission as New Chief." *The Washington Post* (Sept. 30, 1989): Sec. A.

Wolf, Craig. "General Powell Sees the Bronx He Loved, in Memory." *The New York Times* (Apr. 16, 1991): Sec. B.

Woodward, Bob. *The Commanders.* New York: Simon and Schuster, 1991.

———. "The Conversion of General Powell." *The Washington Post* (Dec. 21, 1991): Sec. A.

INDEX

about . . . time magazine, 61
Abrams, Elliot, 45
Afghanistan, 60–61
Air Force, U.S., 68–71, 80
AirLand strategy, 105, 106
Americal Division, 29
Andrews Air Force Base, 95
Angola, 59
Antiwar movement, 28, 30, 85
Apartheid, 61
Arms control negotiations, 43, 49, 55, 57–58
Army Rocks, 112
Army Times, 29
Atlanta Chamber of Commerce, 69

Baker, Lt. Kristin M., 87
Baldwin, James, 15
Black Eagles (play), 110
Black separatism, 16
Blount, James, 61, 62
Booker, Simeon, 44
Boston Globe, 113, 115
Botha, P. W., 61
Britain, 96, 102, 103, 117–18

Brookings Institution, 71
Browne, Ron, 117
Browne v. Topeka Board of Education (1954), 16, 21
Brubaker, Lee, 39
Buffalo Soldiers, 39, 67
Bush, George, 55–56, 64–67, 69, 71, 75, 77, 79, 82, 87, 92–95, 98, 101, 102, 104–5, 109–11, 115, 118, 119

Canada, 60
Canal Zone, 74
Carlucci, Frank C., 34, 42, 46–50, 53, 57
Carter, Jimmy, 75
Central Intelligence Agency (CIA), 48, 50, 57, 84, 94
Cheney, Richard B., 69–70, 76, 77, 80–82, 93, 98, 102, 116
City College of New York (CCNY), 11–19, 33
Civil Rights Act (1964), 22, 26, 28
Civil rights movement, 21–23

Civil War, The (PBS series), 118
Cold War, end of, 86, 88
Colombia, 74, 75
Communism, failure of, 69, 86
Congress, U.S., 30, 37, 45, 88, 95, 102, 104
Congress of Racial Equality (CORE), 22
Contras, 44-45, 60
Cooper, Gary, 118
Crowe, Adm. William, 69, 101
Custer, Gen. George Armstrong, 27

Daily, Tom, 80
Davis, Gen. Benjamin O., Jr., 15, 68
Davis, Gen. Benjamin O., Sr., 14-15, 68
Defense Department, U.S., 41-45, 50, 75, 93
de Kalb, F. W., 61
Delvalle, Eric Arturo, 75
Democratic party, 55, 116, 117
Depression, 3, 7
Desert One, 75
Desert Sabre, 110
Desert Shield, 93-99
Desert Storm, 104-11, 114
Douglass, Frederick, 69
Dugan, Gen. Michael, 96
Dukakis, Michael, 55-56
Dunne, Colin, 118

Ebony magazine, 26, 44, 81
Eisenhower, Dwight D., 14, 99, 116

Emerson College, 19
Endara, Guillermo, 82
Episcopal church, 7-8
Equal Employment Opportunity Commission, 28

Federal Bureau of Investigation (FBI), 57
Fitzwater, Marlin, 82
Flipper, Lt. Henry O., 72
Forbes magazine, 86
Ford, Gerald R., 37
Ford, Guillermo "Billy," 76
Fort Benning, 17, 25, 27
Fort Bragg, 17, 22
Fort Campbell, 37
Fort Carson, 38
Fort Devens, 19, 22
Fort Leavenworth, 27-29, 38-39
Fort McNair, 37
Fort McPherson, 66, 69
France, 96, 103
Frisby, Michael K., 113, 117

Gaines & Co., 7
George Mason University, 117
Georgetown University, 51
George Washington University, 33
Ginzberg & Co., 7
Glaspie, April, 89
Goldwater-Nichols Reorganization Act (1986), 70-71
Grant, Cary, 118
Grenada, U.S. invasion of, 43, 75
Griscom, Thomas, 51, 56

Guatemala, 60
Gulf War, 89–111, 113, 114

Haiti, 60
Helms, Jesse, 116
Herres, Gen. Robert T., 69–70
Horn of Africa, 59
Howard University, 53
Hughes, Langston, 16, 68
Hussein, Saddam, 89, 92–94, 96–97, 100–101, 103–4, 106–11

Intermediate Range Nuclear Forces Treaty, 55, 60, 64
Iran-contra scandal, 45–49
Iran hostage crisis, 75
Iraq, 89–111
Iraqi-Iranian War, 92
Israel, 92, 95, 109

Jackson, Derrick Z., 115–16
Jackson, Jesse, 116, 117
James Reese Europe American Legion, 53
Jet magazine, 38
"Jim Crow" laws, 22
Johnson, Lyndon, 30, 35
Joint Chiefs of Staff, 49, 66–72, 75, 76, 81, 87, 101, 107, 116, 119
Joint Operations Training Center, 83
Jordan, 94
Just Cause, 80–84

Kester, John, 37–38
King, Martin Luther, Jr., 22, 63, 69
Kissinger, Henry, 49

Korb, Lawrence, 71
Korea, 34–36
Korean War, 14–16
Kurds, 92
Kuwait, 89, 92–96, 100, 102, 106, 109, 111

Lebanon, 42, 75
Little Bighorn, Battle of, 27
London Times, 118
Lopez, Elliott, 114

Major, John, 102
Malcolm X, 16
Mandela, Nelson, 61
Marines, U.S., 42–43, 70, 75, 79, 106
Moiseyev, Gen. Mikhail A., 97–98
Montgomery bus boycott, 22
Morris High School, 10–11, 113

National Association of Black Journalists, 67
National Guard, 66
National Military Command Center, 94
National Press Club, 88
National Security Council (NSC), 34, 48–51, 56–58, 60, 65, 76, 102
National War College, 37
Nation of Islam, 16
NATO, 60, 62
Naval Academy, 80
Navy, U.S., 43, 70
New York Times, The, 108
New York University, 11
Nicaragua, 44–46, 60

Nixon, Richard M., 34, 35, 37, 49
Noriega, Manuel, 45, 74–80, 82–86
North, Oliver, 46
North Carolina Agricultural and Technical College, 22
Nuclear weapons, 62–63, 92
Nunn, Sam, 101

Office of Management and Budget, 34
Organization of American States, 84

Panama, 45, 60, 73–85, 87, 93
Parks, Rosa, 22
PBS, 118
Peck, Gregory, 118
Pérez de Cuéllar, Javier, 103
Pershing Rifles, 14
Persian Gulf, 60
war in, see Gulf War
Philippines, 60
Poindexter, John, 46
Powell, Alma Johnson, 19–20, 22–23, 25–27, 50, 76, 81, 118
Powell, Annmarie, 66
Powell, Gen. Colin Luther
appointed chairman of Joint Chiefs of Staff, 66–72, 75, 76
in Birmingham, 25–27
birth of, 4
British and, 117–18
celebrity status of, 118–19
childhood of, 4–8
in college, 11–19

at Command and General Staff College, 28
education of, 8–11
enlistment in Army of, 18–19
at Fort Leavenworth, 27–29, 38–39
in graduate school, 33
hobbies of, 118
and Iran-contra scandal, 45–49
in Korea, 34–36
marriage of, 19–20
as National Security Adviser, 53–65
and National Security Council, 48–51
at National War College, 37
and Panama, 73, 75–85
at Pentagon, 33, 36–38
and Persian Gulf War, 89–111
in politics, 115–17
and racial issues, 112–15
in ROTC, 14, 16–18
rules for daily guidance of, 72–73
and son's injury, 50–51
in Vietnam, 21–25, 28–33, 40
Weinberger and, 39, 41–45
in West Germany, 19, 45–47
West Point graduation address by, 87–88
as White House Fellow, 34
Powell, Linda, 32, 66, 118–19
Powell, Luther Theophilus, 1–5, 7
Powell, Marilyn, 4, 6, 8

INDEX ★ 149

Powell, Maude McCoy, 1–10
Powell, Michael, 23, 25, 50–51, 66
Powell, Sir Charles, 117

Randolph, Gen. Bernard B., 67–68
Reagan, Ronald, 44–45, 47–49, 52, 53, 55–59, 61, 64–65, 75, 76, 92, 115
Republican party, 34, 52, 64, 115–17
Reserve Officers Training Corps (ROTC), 14, 16–18, 87
Reversal of Fortune (movie), 118–19
Revolutionary War, 15
Riots, 28
Robinson, Gen. Roscoe, 67
Roosevelt, Franklin D., 15
Roosevelt, Theodore, 67
Roque, Victor, 10

Santayana, George, 97
Saudi Arabia, 92–96, 98, 99, 103, 104, 106
Schwarzkopf, Gen. H. Norman, 93, 99, 104, 106, 108
Segregation, 15–17, 22
Senate, U.S., 76
　Armed Services Committee, 87, 95, 101
Shultz, George, 44, 57–58
Smullen, Col. Frederic W., II, 109
Smullen, Col. William, III, 80
South Africa, 61, 63, 86

Southern Christian Leadership Conference, 71
Soviet Union, 43, 46, 49, 55, 57–58, 60–62, 78, 86, 88, 97–98, 103
Spanish American War, 67
St. Margaret's Episcopal Church, 8
St. Phillip's Episcopal Church, 2, 4
Starks, Tiffani, 80–81
Starr, Roger, 108
Star Wars program, 55
State Department, U.S., 44, 50, 52, 57
Strategic Defense Initiative, 55
Strear, Mitchell, 16–17
Supreme Court, 15, 21
Syria, 43

Taylor, William J., 106
Tet Offensive, 32
Thatcher, Margaret, 117
Thucydides, 72
Thurman, Gen., 82–84
Time magazine, 31–32
Tower, John, 48

United Nations, 92, 98, 100, 103, 111
　Security Council, 96
U.S. News & World Report, 108

Veterans of Foreign Wars, 111
Vietnam War, 21–25, 28–33, 35, 40, 62, 75, 78, 79, 85, 87, 98, 100, 101

Voter Registration Act (1965), 28
Vuono, Gen. Carl, 65, 108

Wall Street Journal, The, 85
Walter Reed Army Medical Center, 50
War on Poverty, 35
Watson, Spann, 71
Webster, William, 84
Weinberger, Caspar, 34, 39, 41–45, 48, 49, 53, 58, 62, 86
Wembley, Sgt. Addison, 111
West Germany, 19, 45–47
West Point, 15, 19, 68, 72, 87–88
Wicker, Tom, 115
Wilkerson, Larry, 72
Wilkins, Patricia, 117
Wilkins, Roger, 117
William and Mary College, 66
Williams, Pete, 108–9
World War II, 5, 7, 14, 15, 93–94, 110, 113, 116